Sustainable Business in the Era of Digital Transformation

Sustainable development is a complex issue and despite many studies and publications in recent years, it remains poorly recognised on best practices in core business areas. Achieving the Sustainable Development Goals in accordance with the 2030 Agenda for Sustainable Development depends on research and innovation. Therefore, the transition to sustainable development requires investment in technology, new business models, and social and environmental innovations that contribute to shaping new business and promoting sustainable business practices.

This book seeks to understand how sustainability affects core business areas, with a focus on strategic and entrepreneurial activities. Given these considerations, the main purpose of this book is twofold: (1) to contribute to a better understanding of important and current trends in the field of sustainable transformation in core business areas; and (2) to provide a comprehensive overview of quantitative and qualitative studies in the field. The book ultimately seeks to shed light on how companies are implementing sustainable transformation in the core areas of product and marketing, entrepreneurship, and innovation, which is supported by appropriate project management strategies.

The book provides researchers and upper-level students in economics, business, and other social sciences with an overview of interdisciplinary theoretical and conceptual perspectives and frameworks for successful business transformation. It will be of particular value to those researching sustainable development and strategic management.

Mariusz Sołtysik, Associate Professor, Krakow University of Economics. Participant of the Techmatstrateg Strategic Research and Development Program. Contractor in projects financed by the National Science Center and the National Center for Research and Development, including the Leader programme. Contractor in the Horizon 2020 program. Research interests: strategic management, project management, and innovation in the enterprise.

Magdalena Wojnarowska, Associate Professor, Head of the Department of Technology and Ecology of Products at the Krakow University of Economics (KUE). Completed postgraduate studies: Head of Scientific Research and Development Works. An expert in the selection of projects to be co-financed from EU funds in the field of environmental protection. Representative of UEK at KT

270 for Environmental Management of the Polish Committee for Standardization. KUE representative in the Life Science Cluster. Manager and contractor of research projects financed by the following institutions: Minister of Science and Higher Education, National Science Centre, National Center for Research and Development and European H2020.

Maria Urbaniec, Associate Professor and Head of the Department of Entrepreneurship and Innovation at the Krakow University of Economics (Poland). She completed her PhD in Economics at the International Graduate School Zittau of the Technische Universitat Dresden (Germany). She is a member of international scientific societies such as the European Council for Small Business and Entrepreneurship (ECSB). In 2021, she was elected vice-president of the Polish Economic Society. She has authored over 150 scientific papers in academic journals and monographs. Her research interests include sustainable entrepreneurship, eco-innovation, sustainable development, the labour market, and the digital economy.

Vesna Zabkar, Professor of Marketing at the School of Economics and Business, University of Ljubljana (SEB LU) and a former Vice-Dean of Research and Doctoral Studies at SEB LU. She was a visiting scholar at Northwestern University (Fulbright Grant) and is a visiting professor at the University of Vienna (Chair of International Marketing). Her research interests focus on sustainability, marketing accountability, and international marketing. Her work has been published in the Journal of Business Ethics, British Journal of Management, Journal of Business Research, Industrial Marketing Management, Journal of International Marketing, European Management Review, Journal of Service Management, and other outlets.

Marek Ćwiklicki, Prof. Dr Habil., Prof. at the Cracow University of Economics. He is Habilitated Doctor of Economics and holds a PhD in Economics in the field of Management Science, both obtained from the Cracow University of Economics in Poland. As Head of the Department of Public Management, he researches, writes, and lectures on organisation theory, business research methodology, and public management. He is also a Member of the Advisory Board of the Research Competence Centre for Corporate Social Responsibility at the FOM University of Applied Sciences in Germany (FOM KompetenzCentrum für Corporate Social Responsibility).

Erica Varese, Associate Professor in the Faculty of Management, University of Turin (Italy). Her main research area is commodity science. She has published articles in many peer-reviewed journals, as well as books and presented papers at international conferences. She is a member of the International Society for Commodity Science and Technology (IGWT), the Accademia Italiana di Scienze Merceologiche (Italian Academy of Commodity Science), and the Academic Academy of the Accademia di Agricoltura di Torino (Agricultural University of Turin – IT).

Routledge Advances in Management and Business Studies

Technologies and Trends in the Halal Industry
Edited by Nor Aida Abdul Rahman, Kamran Mahroof and Azizul Hassan

Digital Transformation, Perspective Development, and Value Creation
Research Case Studies
Edited by Małgorzata Pańkowska

Responsible Management and Sustainable Consumption
Creating a Consumer and Enterprise Social Responsibility Index
Edited by Piotr Wachowiak, Anna Dąbrowska, Monika Zajkowska and Celina Sołek-Borowska

Co-operative and Mutual Enterprises Research
A Comprehensive Overview
Tim Mazzarol

Corruption and the Management of Public Safety
The Governance of Technological Systems
Simon Ashley Bennett

Hofstede Matters
Edited by Sławomir Magala, Christiane Erten, Roger Matthew Bell, Marie-Therese Claes, Senem Yazici and Atila Karabag

Entrepreneurship Education and Internationalisation
Cases, Collaborations and Contexts
Edited by Robert James Crammond and Denis Hyams-Ssekasi

Sustainable Business in the Era of Digital Transformation
Strategic and Entrepreneurial Perspectives
Mariusz Sołtysik, Magdalena Wojnarowska, Maria Urbaniec, Vesna Zabkar, Marek Ćwiklicki and Erica Varese

For more information about this series, please visit: www.routledge.com/Routledge-Advances-in-Management-and-Business-Studies/book-series/SE0305

Sustainable Business in the Era of Digital Transformation

Strategic and Entrepreneurial Perspectives

Mariusz Sołtysik, Magdalena Wojnarowska, Maria Urbaniec, Vesna Zabkar, Marek Ćwiklicki and Erica Varese

Routledge
Taylor & Francis Group
LONDON AND NEW YORK

First published 2024
by Routledge
4 Park Square, Milton Park, Abingdon, Oxon OX14 4RN

and by Routledge
605 Third Avenue, New York, NY 10158

Routledge is an imprint of the Taylor & Francis Group, an informa business

British Library Cataloguing-in-Publication Data
A catalogue record for this book is available from the British Library

ISBN: 978-1-032-69784-0 (hbk)
ISBN: 978-1-032-69787-1 (pbk)
ISBN: 978-1-032-69789-5 (ebk)

DOI: 10.4324/9781032697895

Typeset in Times New Roman
by Deanta Global Publishing Services, Chennai, India

Contents

Introduction

Sustainability is a complex issue and despite many studies and publications in recent years, it remains poorly recognised in terms of best practices in key business areas. Achieving the Sustainable Development Goals (SDGs) in line with the 2030 Agenda for Sustainable Development depends on research and innovation. Therefore, the transition to sustainability requires investments in technology, new business models, and social and environmental innovations that contribute to shaping new businesses and promoting sustainable business practices.

Recent research shows that companies can achieve a competitive advantage if they meet economic, social, and environmental requirements. Sustainability, on the other hand, depends on business activities that are largely market-driven and dependent on sustainable business strategies. These practices become the driving force behind sustainable dynamic capabilities by incorporating environmentally conscious decision-making and the development of sustainability-oriented products, ultimately leading to a competitive advantage. Therefore, researchers say that sustainable business strategies affect the sustainability of organisations.

As a result, there is a growing need for companies to create business opportunities that are aligned with sustainability principles. The main challenge for companies in terms of strategic development is to find a balance between economic benefits and environmental responsibility, and ultimately to achieve the sustainable development goals, taking into account social needs. Companies are under increasing pressure on the one hand to grow and maximise shareholder returns, and on the other hand, they are under pressure from society to ensure that their products and services are environmentally friendly and responsible. Therefore, it is important to align your core business activities with the sustainable management of natural resources and the manufacture of products, using products in a way that does not endanger the environment and society, while at the same time providing a competitive advantage. To meet these demands and achieve long-term sustainability, companies are entrepreneurial, i.e. they are looking for new solutions and creating sustainable innovations or new value in economic, social, and environmental terms.

Given the above considerations, the main purpose of this book is twofold: (1) to contribute to a better understanding of important and current trends in the field of sustainable transformation in key business areas and (2) to provide a comprehensive overview of quantitative and qualitative research in the field.

DOI: 10.4324/9781032697895-1

These research objectives will contribute to answering the main research question on how companies implement sustainability transformation strategies and practices in their key business areas.

The book's approach provides scholars and students of economics, business, and other social sciences with an overview of interdisciplinary theoretical and conceptual perspectives and frameworks for successful business transformation. In particular, it presents a comprehensive range of research on key areas of sustainable business such as product and marketing, entrepreneurship, and innovation, which are supported by appropriate project management strategies. The scope of the issues covered is also tailored to the needs of business practitioners who want to understand the changes taking place in modern business as a result of sustainable transformation.

With a focus on sustainable transformation, this book seeks to understand how sustainability impacts core business areas. These effects include changes in various strategic and entrepreneurial activities. This phenomenon has both positive and negative implications for businesses.

Based on these objectives, *the following research questions* will be answered:

- How are companies implementing sustainability transformation strategies and practices in their key business areas?
- What are the factors that determine sustainable business transformation?
- What strategies support sustainable business transformation?
- How do companies shape strategic and entrepreneurial actions for sustainable development: Are they based on single sustainable actions (innovation projects) or do these activities focus on strategic sustainable actions?
- What are the features of sustainability transformation and what challenges does it pose for companies?

The monograph consists of seven chapters.

The first chapter, entitled *Sustainable business transformation: Origins*, points out that technological progress and widespread access to modern technologies pose challenges for organisations related to achieving sustainable business operations. In the context of global climate change and environmental degradation, the transition to sustainable development is becoming a key goal. Organisations are increasingly paying attention to business strategies that take into account economic, social, and environmental aspects, and the UN Sustainable Development Goals (SDGs) are a determinant of action on the international stage.

The solution may be the implementation of a circular economy, promoting the reuse, repair, and recycling of products, becoming essential to reduce waste and achieve sustainable production. Sustainable entrepreneurship, based on innovation, is a key element in the pursuit of sustainable development, especially for small and medium-sized enterprises.

The chapter points out that sustainable business transformation encompasses an organisation's ability to adapt and rebuild resources in a dynamic environment. The transition to sustainability requires collaboration across sectors of society, and the effectiveness of the circular economy requires testing and life-cycle assessment by design. The ultimate goal is to achieve a balance between economic benefits and environmental responsibility, contributing to the strategic goal of sustainable development.

Chapter 2, *Designing a sustainable business*, points out that designing a sustainable business requires first and foremost defining the importance and consequences of incorporating sustainability as an organisational concept in business. The idea of sustainability rooted in the organisation's mission differentiates the standard profit-oriented business model from the sustainable business model. It can be seen as minimising the activities of enterprises and the consumption and disposal of consumer products in the environment. Hence, two lines of theoretical consideration: What can be done to make a company operating in a given ecosystem more environmentally friendly and how can the results of the company's activities (i.e. products and services) be designed, recycled, used, and so on, to neutralise their impact?

Chapter 3, *Sustainable product*, attention will be focused on defining a sustainable product and analysing the differences compared with an organic product. Attention will be paid both to the design stage, taking into account the role of ecodesign, and to the production of a sustainable product. The key task is to create ecologically safe products and services. This is achieved by making products eco-friendly by design, including recycling, i.e. reducing the production of natural raw materials and maximising the use of secondary raw materials while achieving the highest possible level of recycling at the end of the product's life cycle. Therefore, it is important to design waste with specific properties that can be reused in the production process or used by others.

Chapter 4, *Sustainable marketing*, covers the concept of sustainable marketing, which aims to integrate the ecological, social, and economic dimensions, emerging with a growing interest in environmental issues. The basis of the new approach is a responsible view of how to meet the current needs of consumers, which at the same time will maintain or even increase the ability to meet the needs of the wider society. The chapter deals with the topic of transition from traditional to innovative marketing management based on the implementation of the concept of sustainable marketing in an organisation. Changing the approach to creating new goods and services – the way the company creates, delivers, and communicates its offer, as well as the principles of cooperation with suppliers and customers, are the basis for increasing the level of innovation and minimising the negative impact of business activity on society. Marketing should be the main source and focal point of a company's focus on sustainability. Therefore, the analysis and evaluation of the concept of marketing management in relation to the idea of sustainable development is the main objective of this chapter. The chapter will also present the process of planning and implementing all elements of the marketing mix in such a way as to meet consumer needs and achieve business goals without a negative impact on the environment. In addition, marketing activities undertaken by companies in the context of sustainable development will be characterised, including responsible marketing, green marketing, and social marketing. The aim of this chapter is to operationalise the concept of sustainable marketing. Particular attention will be paid to the tools used in sustainable marketing.

Chapter 5, Sustainable entrepreneurship, presents a model in which, in order to achieve a long-term sustainability effect, companies undertake entrepreneurial activities that are reflected in the search for new solutions and the creation of innovation or new value in economic, social, and environmental aspects, in addition to solving existing problems. Attention will be directed to the role of entrepreneurship in sustainable development as a new concept of discovering, creating, and exploiting opportunities for (future) goods and services that simultaneously support the natural and social environment and bring economic and non-economic benefits to others. It will be particularly important to highlight that sustainable entrepreneurship can address the challenges of sustainability through various strategies and actions. Driven by social responsibility, companies strive to achieve environmental goals that go beyond legal requirements and commit to achieving better environmental performance. This chapter explores a variety of research into the conceptual framework of sustainable entrepreneurship that drives the transformation of sustainable business.

In Chapter 6, *Sustainable innovation*, an attempt was made to answer the main objective of the question: To what extent is sustainable innovation a part of business strategy? This part assumes that to achieve a long-term sustainability effect, companies undertake entrepreneurial activities that translate into the search for new solutions and the creation of innovation or new value in the economic, social, and environmental dimensions, in addition to solving existing problems. Innovation creates new practices and leads to changes in organisational structures and people's actions. The chapter will point out that sustainable innovation has its roots in sustainable development and is based on ethical, social, economic, and environmental principles. Similar principles can be seen in eco-innovation, agile innovation, and engineering, as well as in the development of thinking about shared values.

Chapter 7, *Sustainable project management,* presents an integrated approach to project management, taking into account sustainable practices and their inclusion in the strategy of ongoing projects in order to ensure the long-term development and success of the organisation. In addition, this chapter will show how sustainably managed projects not only produce concrete results for companies but also have a positive impact on environmental and social aspects. This chapter aims to present a project management model based on sustainability.[1]

1 The publication presents the result of Project No. 057/ZZS/2023/POT financed by a subsidy granted to the University of Economics in Krakow

1 Sustainable business transformation

Origins

Rapid technological advances over the past few decades have increased organisational efficiency, but at the same time, they have created higher expectations for sustainable business operations (Ruiz-Mercader et al., 2006). Moreover, unlike in the past when only a few organisations had access to the latest technologies, today, organisations have relatively broad access to technology (Chen et al., 2019). However, this state of affairs has made them sceptical about technology investments because they do not allow them to achieve a sustainable competitive advantage (Dubey et al., 2019). Therefore, the way to achieve this advantage is through sustainable development by implementing economic, social, and environmental requirements (Jabbour et al., 2018). Stability depends on business activity (Pfeffer, 2010), which is largely driven by new strategies. Sustainable business strategies are also essential for developing the right capabilities that can ensure sustainable business transformation (Gupta et al., 2020).

The phenomenon of "transformation" as a change in the essential conditions of action and decision-making has gained significant importance in economic and social sciences in recent years. In the face of far-reaching global climate change and environmental degradation, the transition to more sustainable development is becoming increasingly important, accompanied in part by enormous challenges faced by economic, political, and social actors.

The implementation of sustainable development is associated with a fundamental change in management methods, taking into account systemic and integrated interdisciplinary approaches (Urbaniec 2015). The need to change the current model of economic development to a more sustainable one has been identified as one of the priority areas not only by the United Nations (UN) but also by the Organisation for Economic Co-operation and Development (OECD) and the European Union (EU). Sustainability is a concept that is gaining popularity as a new trend in socio-economic development around the world. In both politics and industry, there is a growing interest in fostering a sustainable economy in the context of ever-changing conditions for socio-economic development.

Intensified action at the international level is also reflected in the new Sustainable Development Goals set at the UN level as part of the new document-based development agenda entitled "Transforming Our World: The 2030 Agenda for Global Action", adopted at the UN Summit in New York on 25 September 2015 (UN 2015). The programme sets out 17 headline objectives and 169 related tasks. Some

DOI: 10.4324/9781032697895-2

of the goals (e.g. goals 8, 9, and 12) relate directly to sustainability at the company level. These objectives emphasise the promotion of development policy supporting production activities, entrepreneurship, creativity, and innovation conducive to the development of micro, small, and medium-sized enterprises, as well as the introduction of sustainable development of industry by increasing the efficiency of the use of resources and the use and application of clean and environmentally friendly technologies and production processes.

Therefore, there is a need for a global transition to an environmentally friendly economy (a green or circular economy). The green economy cannot be imposed from above but must be developed by entrepreneurs who respond to political incentives by implementing innovations in management and technology. Green products and technologies are finally being brought to market by entrepreneurs who implement ideas, turning prototypes into profitable, environmentally friendly products.

In the era of intensive development of the knowledge-based economy, enterprises are increasingly strengthening their competitive position through innovative activities in the field of sustainable development or corporate social responsibility (Lin et al., 2015).

It is worth noting that the economy of the last 150 years has been based on a one-way model (take, make, use, and dispose), which was characterised by the extraction of resources for production and consumption and the absence of plans for the reuse of waste or active regeneration of the economy (Venkata Mohan et al., 2016). Over time, it has been documented that this linear economic model is responsible for a number of problems, mainly related to the fact that:

- virgin materials are extracted more quickly than the replenishment capacity;
- after use, products are often dumped in landfills or processed in incinerators, resulting in valuable and scarce natural resources being extracted – and thus lost – to produce new products;
- hazardous waste management, which often characterises linear management, leads to the formation of hazardous substances that leach into soil, water, and air, thus causing alarming environmental pollution conditions;
- the production and transportation of products are responsible for significant energy consumption and environmental pollution.

As such, linear economies can be considered completely unsustainable in both environmental, economic, and social dimensions (Ingrao et al., 2018; Korhonen, Nuur, et al., 2018).

In this context, the circular economy could be an important alternative, as it would help keep products, components, and materials at the highest levels of utility and value (Ingrao et al., 2021; Webster, 2020).

Adopting a circular approach to products has great potential for sustainability in the broadest sense of the word, with the resulting benefits for people, planet, and well-being. A sustainable circular economy is about designing and promoting products that are sustainable and can be reused, repaired, and refurbished before being recycled. This aspect is prioritised in the implementation of circular economy models, as it best preserves the functional value of products rather than just recovering the material or energy content and constantly reinventing products. The circular economy actually determines how to reuse, repair, and recycle items, thereby reducing waste and, in general, increasing sustainable production and consumption. In addition, this approach saves energy and helps to avoid irreversible damage to the environment caused by the extraction and use of resources at a rate exceeding the Earth's capacity to replenish them (EU, 2019).

Sustainable products have a long lifespan and can be repaired, even multiple times when they break. When a consumer no longer needs a product, it is passed on – and thus reused – by another consumer. This is what happens in the second-hand market, where products are updated or renewed and, in a sense, are reborn to a second life after a technical or economic one. When this is not possible, their materials are recycled and only a minimal portion goes to energy recovery (EU, 2019).

During production and use, products generally use the minimum amount of resources, such as energy or water, necessary to perform their functions (EU, 2019).

Based on ecodesign, consumer products such as food, beverages, cosmetics, and detergents should be produced with minimal impact on resources and should be consumed with as little waste as possible. In addition, action needs to be taken to minimise environmental emissions and climate impacts throughout the life cycle (EU, 2019). According to the EU (2019), this would lead to less resource consumption, less waste, more jobs in the repair and recycling sectors, and financial savings, while preserving product-related services.

Products obtained from such circular economy production systems can be considered more sustainable than conventional products (EU, 2019). Therefore, in light of the above, there is evidence that the circular economy can contribute to improving the sustainability of products and services from a life-cycle perspective. This can be considered one of the main reasons why the circular economy is of great interest to researchers, policymakers, and managers (Hysa et al., 2020). Geissdoerfer et al. (2017) highlighted that the circular economy is a prerequisite for sustainable development because it acts as a regenerative system that minimises material and energy inputs, as well as emissions and waste. However, it is desirable that measures targeting the circular economy are tested using tools such as life cycle sustainability assessment (LCSA) and life cycle assessment (LCA) already at the design stage so that the circular economy can be truly effective in ensuring the overall sustainability of material goods and from a life-cycle perspective (Ingrao et al., 2021).

In order to achieve a long-term sustainability effect, enterprises, especially in the SME area, undertake entrepreneurial activities, which are reflected in the search for new solutions and the creation of innovation or new value in economic, social, and environmental terms, as well as in solving existing problems (Johnson and Schaltegger, 2019; Muñoz & Cohen, 2018; Sarango-Lalangui et al., 2018). Therefore, innovation as a source of sustainable entrepreneurship is essential.

From an economic point of view, the role of entrepreneurship in sustainable development is seen as a new concept of discovering, creating, and seizing opportunities for (future) goods and services that simultaneously sustain the natural and social environment and provide economic and non-economic benefits to others (Johnson & Schalteger, 2019; Patzelt and Shepherd, 2011; Muñoz & Cohen, 2018). Entrepreneurship has the potential to address market failures in a market economy, in particular with regard to environmental issues.

Sustainable entrepreneurship can address sustainability challenges through a variety of strategies and activities. Driven by social responsibility, companies strive to achieve environmental goals that go beyond legal requirements and are also committed to achieving better environmental performance. While some researchers argue that strategies that support sustainability generate additional costs and reduce the productivity of firms (Palmer et al., 1995), other researchers explain that these strategies create a competitive advantage by implementing more efficient processes, increasing productivity, reducing costs, and creating new market opportunities (Wagner, 2009). Environmental impact must be embedded in the overall process of improving productivity and competitiveness. The resource productivity model, not the pollution control model, should guide the strategic decision-making process in enterprises. It should be noted that sustainable entrepreneurship is a new paradigm of business development based on the concept of sustainable development.

Sustainable development cannot be achieved without transforming consumer societies into sustainable ones because, on the one hand, increased demand increases sales of goods and services, which brings profits to businesses, and on the other hand, it indirectly has a negative impact on the ecosystem. Therefore, balancing economic goals with environmental and social goals is a major challenge not only for today's producers, manufacturers, and consumers, but also for governments, social organisations, and other economic actors (Eisenmenger et al., 2020).

As such, sustainable business transformation has been assumed to refer to the ability of enterprises to acquire and rebuild internal and external organisational resources, including environmental (ecological) and technological resources, in order to cope with a changing business environment and by becoming path-dependent and creating new organisational resources and strategic practices (Eisenhardt & Martin, 2000; Wohlgemuth & Wenzel, 2016). These transition processes actively support circular strategies and eco-innovation practices in a turbulent business environment and are one of the sources of competitive advantage for companies (Dangelico et al., 2015). The main goal of sustainable enterprises is to achieve a balance between economic benefits and environmental responsibility, thereby achieving the strategic goal of sustainable development (Chan et al., 2017; Li et al., 2019; Nguyen et al., 2017).

2 Designing a sustainable business

2.1 Methods of designing a sustainable business

2.1.1 Sustainability as a guiding business logic

Designing a sustainable business first requires establishing the meaning and consequences of incorporating sustainability as an organising concept in business. The sustainability idea embedded in the organisation's mission distinguishes a typical for-profit business model from the sustainable business model (SBM).

The business model explains "the rationale of how an organisation creates, delivers and captures value" (Osterwalder & Pigneur, 2010). The business model canvas depicts its main parts, such as value proposition, value creation, and value capture. Value proposition (products, services, etc.) and value creation logic (activities, resources, etc.) should include sustainability linking the company's internal and external environments (Abdelkafi & Täuscher, 2016). Because sustainability is understood in terms of economic, environmental, and social dimensions (the so-called triple bottom line approach (people, planet, profit) (Bocken et al., 2014)), it means that the sustainable business is responsible for all three aspects of its performance in the long term. Adopting this framework for sustainable business demonstrates the complexity due to the parallel consideration of three dimensions: social, environmental, and economic (Joyce & Paquin, 2016). However, the logic associated with a business model focusing on value is useful for clarification of what it means for a business to transform towards sustainability.

The sustainable business embodies "reducing [the company's] impact on the Earth's life- and eco-systems" (Høgevold & Svensson, 2012). It can be perceived as minimising enterprises' activities and consumer product usage and disposal on the environment. Therefore, two lines of theoretical considerations emerge: what could be done to be more environmentally friendly in a company operating in a given ecosystem and how results of the company's activities (i.e., products and services) can be designed, recycled, utilised, and so on, to neutralise their impact. Those two aspects jointly describe the SBM presented in more detail in Section 2.2 as the result of sustainable design. Another approach is expressed by a transition to SBM explained in Section 2.3.

DOI: 10.4324/9781032697895-3

2.1.2 Sustainable business activities in manufacturing

The sustainable business model archetypes study revealed eight types assigned to technological, social, and organisational spheres (Bocken et al., 2014). These archetypes present the ways of making business sustainable. They matched the dichotomy described above: internal and external business environments.

The first one creates technological innovations represented by the following methods: maximising material and energy efficiency, creating value from waste, and substituting with renewables and natural processes. The Lean approach has already proved to have a positive impact on better waste management and energy efficiency through its tools like the 5S programme, value stream mapping, and Kaizen events (Caldera et al., 2017). Their mastery leads to offering changed products or services. Table 2.1 presents the logic behind them, explaining the approach towards sustainability in each of them and examples of selected methods.

2.1.2.1 Methods for designing sustainable products

Changing the product or service can be done as a result of ecodesign. Ecodesign is defined as "a systematic approach that considers environmental aspects in design and development with the aim to reduce adverse environmental impacts

Table 2.1 Three sustainable business model archetypes for manufactures

Archetype	*Logic behind*	*Examples*
Maximising material and energy efficiency	A lower use of resources will create less waste, pollution, and emissions.	• Lean manufacturing • Additive manufacturing • Low carbon manufacturing
Creating value from waste	Changing thinking about waste as a resource that can be re-used by others, which reduces the landfill and diminishes the demand for primary resources.	• Industrial symbiosis • Closed-loop business models • Recycling • Cradle-2-Cradle
Substituting with renewables and natural processes	Replacing conventional resources with renewable alternatives and adopting natural processes results in vastly more eco-friendly industrial operations, resulting in minimising the environmental impact.	• Blue Economy • Zero Emission initiatives • Local renewable energy solutions (solar, windmills)

Source: Based on Bocken et al. (2014).

throughout the life cycle of a product" (ISO, 2020, p. 14). The ecodesign procedure resembles the traditional design process but requires more time for environmental assessment (Vallet et al., 2013). For this purpose, different specific tools are created like life cycle assessment (LCA), life cycle costing, or eco-matrix, which are also supported by computer software.

2.1.3 Sustainable business activities for society

A group classified as a social archetype represents focus on functionality, engagement with stakeholders, and encouraging sufficiency. These methods benefit from close cooperation with customers and stakeholders, offering better fulfilment of needs. Delivering functionality over ownership leaves companies with better control over products and resources required to sustain them. Bocken et al. (2014) point out a re-use of materials and enhanced product longevity as results of this SBM. The effects are achieved differently compared with innovation in the manufacturing process described earlier. Such results also appear when organisations are focused on long-term health and well-being (Bocken et al., 2014). This is achieved through certification processes aimed at undertaking new activities beneficial for society or the environment. Eco-labels can impact consumer behaviours, leading to changes in production methods (Wojnarowska et al., 2021). The last archetype qualified as social refers to reducing consumption. This approach is less obvious compared with the previous ones. It refers to consumer behaviours related to pro-environmental attitudes, like buying second-hand things (Bocken et al., 2014).

2.1.3.1 Methods for designing sustainable business for society

The product life cycle is a useful concept allowing the tracing of potential to implement sustainability into a product. The design, manufacturing, distribution, usage, maintenance, disposal, disassembly, recycling, re-use, and so on offer new ways of thinking (Niemann et al., 2009; Tao & Yu, 2018) and are the subject of study where many methods can be used (see Table 2.1).

The transformational activities refer to changes in manufacturing technology that require fewer resources and less energy, promoting sustainability among the company's customers and stakeholders (Hernández-Chea et al., 2021). For this purpose, adding servitisation and digitalisation to offered products creates the product-service system (Alcayaga et al., 2019) or service-oriented business models. An integrated offer enriches the value delivered to customers but also helps to extend product usability (Bressanelli et al., 2017).

2.1.4 Organisation for sustainable business

The above methods of embedding sustainability in business complete organisational changes represented by a business mission oriented towards simultaneous focus on benefit, society, and environment and the search for scaling up existing sustainable solutions. Delivering social value or shareholder value (Ćwiklicki &

O'Riordan, 2017) can impact the internal organisational setting like introducing the methods described as sustainable business model archetypes for manufacturing. The examples of this approach are different not-for-profit legal and organisational forms like social enterprise and hybrid organisations (Doherty et al., 2014; Smith et al., 2013). Scaling can work for this purpose as well as maximising benefits for society. It can be done via licensing, franchising, open innovation, and crowd sourcing (Bocken et al., 2014).

2.1.4.1 Methods for designing a sustainable business model

Designing organisational solutions aimed at repurposing for society and the environment and scaling up comprises of embedding hybridity into the organisational mission. The listed organisational forms by Bocken et al. (2014), social enterprises, cooperatives, and collectives, demonstrate a social mission as dominant or equal to the economic purpose. Such forms are chosen due to the existing supporting regulatory and financial setting in a given country (Urmanaviciene & Praakli, 2021). Social business ventures can be based on micro distribution and retail, experience-based customer credit, last-mile grid utilities, smallholder procurement, value-for-money degrees and housing, and e-transaction platforms (Lüdeke-Freund et al., 2016).

The methods of designing a sustainable organisation refer to the same as for sustainable business model design (Baldassarre et al., 2020). They refer to the business models canvas adding new aspects of experimentation and innovation (see Chapter 6). Other sustainable business model design tools listed by Hope (2018) create two groups. The first group consists of general strategic management methods like SWOT, PESTLE, portfolio analysis, and so on. The second one creates specific tools based on the business model canvas, frameworks, roadmaps, value analysis tools, and innovation kit/pack for which sustainability serves as the main feature.

Presented above, the sustainable business model archetypes express the ways of achieving sustainability at the level of technology and manufacturing, organisational management, and customer and stakeholder management. These three levels of business show different approaches to designing a sustainable product/service (see Chapter 3) and the ways of delivering them to customers (see Chapter 4). Therefore, the specific methods for creating a sustainable business relate to ecodesign, environmental labelling, or LCA (Wojnarowska et al., 2022). Moving beyond the company's boundaries, the sustainable value proposition concerns marketing activities and market actors like customers, investors and shareholders, suppliers, and partners, community, government, external agencies, media, academia (Bocken et al., 2013).

In this section, the methods for sustainable business design are linked to SBM and its value proposition and value creation. Those activities depend on the sustainable business strategy: sustainable born companies or those orienting their mission towards sustainability, i.e., sustainable business transformation. In the next section, the SBM as the prospective and desired state is explained.

2.2 Concept of sustainable business models

2.2.1 Definition of sustainable business model

An explanation of how organisations can create and deliver sustainable products and services enables the Sustainable Business Model (SBM). In one earlier work dedicated to it, SBM is described as "a model where sustainability concepts shape the driving force of the firm and its decision making" (Stubbs & Cocklin, 2008). Embracing sustainability represents the organisational mission (purpose) where economic, social, and environmental aspects are exposed and measured, while engaging stakeholders and encompassing the systems perspective (ibidem). Table 2.2 presents some SBM definitions identified by Lozano (2018) and Geissdoerfer et al. (2018). Aligning these definitions reveals that "there is no such thing as an absolute SBM (…). Instead, principles/practices that enable a fit with the vision of sustainable development (…) can be incorporated in the BM" (Pieroni et al., 2019). Goni et al. (2021) synthesised the differences among SBM and traditional business models by pointing out that SBM seeks to generate value for multiple stakeholders and the environment, includes non-financial forms of value aside from profit, and considers the negative effect on society and the environment.

Table 2.2 Sustainable business model definitions

Source	*Definition*
(Stubbs & Cocklin, 2008)	"a SBM could be conceptualised in various ways such as a narrative of sustainability practices; a description of features, attributes, and/or characteristics; a list of necessary and sufficient conditions; a representation of business processes; a firm-level description; a systems-level description; or some combinations of these".
(Schaltegger et al., 2016)	"A business model for sustainability helps describing, analysing, managing, and communicating (i) a company's sustainable value proposition to its customers, and all other stakeholders, (ii) how it creates and delivers this value, (iii) and how it captures economic value while maintaining or regenerating natural, social, and economic capital beyond its organizational boundaries".
(Abdelkafi & Täuscher, 2016)	"BMfS [Business Model for Sustainability] enables the firm to reinforce the mutual interdependencies between the value created for its customers and the natural environment as well as the value captured for itself".
(Geissdoerfer et al., 2018)	"business models that incorporate pro-active multi-stakeholder management, the creation of monetary and non-monetary value for a broad range of stakeholders, and hold a long-term perspective".
(Geissdoerfer et al., 2016)	"a simplified representation of the elements, the interrelation between these elements, and the interactions with its stakeholders that an organisational unit uses to create, deliver, capture, and exchange sustainable value for, and in collaboration with, a broad range of stakeholders".

Source: Own elaboration based on Geissdoerfer et al. (2018) and Lozano (2018).

2.2.2 Value proposition

The first section of this chapter presented the typology of sustainable business models without going into the details of its creation and structure. The key element in a business model is value proposition explaining what the organisation delivers to customers, stakeholders, and society. Referring to sustainability, proper amendments need to be inserted into it as follows: "a promise on the economic, environmental and social benefits that a firm's offering delivers to customers and society at large, considering both short-term profits and long-term sustainability" (Patala et al., 2016). According to Baldassarre et al. (2017), the value proposition "allows simultaneous value creation for multiple stakeholders, including customers, shareholders, suppliers and partners as well as the environment and society". The process of creating and developing a sustainable value proposition requires including a triple bottom perspective in assessing the potential impact, identifying customers' value drivers, KPIs, and life-cycle analysis (ibidem). Since sustainability is a novel concept for most companies, it needs to be embedded in business routines. Most literature describes the integration of this concept into business models (Ferlito & Faraci, 2022). The value proposition should express the mission and ethics, explaining the governance model of the company (Baldassarre et al., 2017).

One of the most problematic issues in defining value proposition is inclusion and balancing different, sometimes conflicting, stakeholders' needs and expectations (Morioka et al., 2016). The term coined earlier describes this assumption as a shared value. It means "policies and operating practices that enhance the competitiveness of a company while simultaneously advancing the economic and social conditions in the communities in which it operates" (Porter & Kramer, 2011). This definition, not related to sustainable development literature, reveals the significance of stakeholders and the necessity of cooperation with them. It can be done by implementing technological, social, and organisational innovations (Boons & Lüdeke-Freund, 2013; Morioka et al., 2016).

2.2.3 Value creation and delivery

The second part of the SBM is value creation and delivery. Typically, it covers customer relationships, activities, resources, and partners. Sustainability exposes the requirements for society engagement (customers, stakeholders, workers) and pro-environmental management regarding resources and activities. Early identified sustainable initiatives mainly refer to the environment such as benign emissions, renewable energy, and eliminating waste and closing the loop. Social initiatives relate to compliance with ISO 9001 Quality Management and 14000 Environmental Management standards, and sensitivity hook-up (Stubbs & Cocklin, 2008). The former mentioned SBM for manufacturing archetypes, which reveals value creation as (Bocken et al., 2014):

- using fewer resources and generating less unnecessary industrial waste and emissions polluting the environment associated with production.
- introducing closed-loop recycling (re-use of materials) through close cooperation with customers and supply chain partners.

- increasing a product's life cycle with provision maintenance and upgrading services with durable materials.
- improvements in the manufacturing process and technology, as well as improving the efficiency of the whole value chain.
- using renewable materials and resources for manufacturing.
- modifying and extending partnership for better utilisation of waste and increasing the capacity.

Other types of activities aim at changing consumer behaviour. It recalls the rationalisation of lifestyle (Hobson, 2002). It refers to social influence, habit formation, individual self, feelings and cognition, and tangibility (Pilch & Miśniakiewicz, 2022). Value creation focuses on societal and environmental benefits that cross over the organisational boundaries (Bocken et al., 2014). Therefore, cooperation with different groups of stakeholders is required. For example, a study about energy consumption behaviours revealed that cynicism and materiality have a negative association with such behaviour (Malodia & Bhatt, 2019). What requires undertaking are informational campaigns not only led by energy companies but also other institutional bodies.

2.2.4 Value capture

The final part of SBM refers to value capture, which is associated with impact measuring (Baldassarre et al., 2017). The list of identified areas where measurement was investigated covers the following: sustainability disclosure and performance; determinants of sustainable disclosure; critical environmental accounting; sustainable operations and supply chain management; carbon accounting; and sustainability standards and reporting (Mura et al., 2018). The key findings from studying recent trends call for including stakeholders in performance assessment at different stages of the product life cycle and parts of SBM. It results in complexity of measurement due to embracing specific individuals to a given stakeholder groups approach, treating those groups as an integral part of the assessment process. Mura et al. (2018) give examples of regulatory bodies, certification agencies, external auditors, and so on, which leads to the suggestion to embrace a multi-stakeholder perspective. Then, stakeholders are intentionally involved in designing measures for value capture.

Because value capture is aimed for society, then the social value measurement needs to be demonstrated alongside technical measures like carbon footprints. This social dimension is a consequence of inclusion into value proposition mentioned earlier as long-term health and well-being (Bocken et al., 2014). These qualities are not objective and depend on a given social, institutional, and regulatory settings.

2.3 Model of sustainable business transformation

2.3.1 Assumptions for sustainable business transformation

Current knowledge about sustainable business transformation delivers scarce evidence regarding relations between implementing sustainability and economic performance (Abdelkafi & Täuscher, 2016). If we consider sustainability as limiting the potential of a company, then profit opportunities also decrease. However, interpreting change in business models as a chance opportunity to re-build the business, catching up to recent trends, and so on gives new promises (new value). For that purpose, the phrase "Sustainable Business Model Innovation" or "Business model innovation for sustainability" is used. It underlines the importance of innovation in business renewal. SBMI enables the incorporation of sustainability into business models (Shakeel et al., 2020).

Sustainable business transformation requires changes not only in the company's business models, but also modifications in consumption and production, thus embracing industries and societies (Hernández-Chea et al., 2021). From long-term changes (industry and society) through medium-term (value chain) to short-term (firm level), the model of sustainable business can focus on one or all three time horizons and levels. In this chapter, we tackle all three dimensions with more attention paid to the company level. Aligning these dimensions gives an opportunity to investigate the interplay among economic, legal, political, and global spheres (Heikkurinen et al., 2019). The localisation of change agents in the socio-economic system helps to plan the change.

2.3.2 Micro level (company)

At the company level, the starting point towards sustainable business constitutes its purpose, or mission. The beginning of revising the model can be external pressures coming from business partners, customers, or shareholders. Mixing new ideas with existing business practices requires an attitude encouraging learning and experimenting (Bingham & Davis, 2012). Searching for a new mission is a result of exchanging, transforming, and confronting knowledge from different actors.

Reconfiguration of value propositions can be explained as the result of identification, translation, embeddedness, and sharing new business ideas with business partners (Roome & Louche, 2016). Going through these steps means adding new aspects to the current model but also abandoning those that become obsolete. These changes can be logically developed based on changes in the value proposition (Abdelkafi & Täuscher, 2016).

The above transformation refers to a company level; however, some studies emphasise the role of individual actions and refer to employees' psychological capital (Shan et al., 2023) and employee green behaviour (Unsworth et al., 2021). Understanding the psychological microfoundations (Gond et al., 2017) better explains the transformation process. However, because of a lack of studies about individual drivers of sustainable engagement, this phenomenon can be informed by analysing attitudes and perceptions towards eco-innovations, environmental management, and CSR. Drivers, evaluations, mechanisms of reactions, boundary conditions, and outcomes of reactions can provide details about the learning process (Gond et al., 2017), resulting in time required to adapt to a new business reality.

2.3.3 Mezzo level (business network; supply chain)

Transformation in the supply chain is crucial for sustainable transformation. The former study on circular business model transition revealed that collaboration with stakeholders is required because it helps to change business models towards more complex ideas for new value proposition, product design, and sustainable business strategies (Ćwiklicki & O'Riordan, 2022). Similarly for sustainable business transition the key role is value supply. Sustainable supply chain management is crucial for better material and resource use, re-use, and recycling (Govindan et al., 2016). The transformation process of the supply chain towards sustainability can be managed by applying well-known quality management approaches like PDCA, ARIS, or DMAIC, while maturity development is based on models created for environmental management (Reefke & Sundaram, 2018; Vásquez et al., 2021). A new recent dimension adding to sustainable transition in the supply chain offers digitalisation resulting from Industry 4.0. However, new technology also generates new challenges related to interoperability, virtualisation, decentralisation, real-time capacity, and modularity (Kazancoglu et al., 2023).

Activities at the tactical level embrace creating and maintaining relationships among the company's partners (customers, suppliers, stakeholders, government, etc.) (Hernández-Chea et al., 2021). A more general framework, like sustainable stakeholder value creation (O'Riordan, 2017), could be useful for understanding the different aspects of this cooperation.

2.3.4 Macro level (industries and societies)

The macro level represents social stakeholders such as local communities, governance, employees, and end users (Joyce & Paquin, 2016). This level represents actors such as policymakers and public authorities responsible for financing, legislation, and institutionalising sustainable transformation (Farla et al., 2012). A less recognised dimension for sustainable business transition is so-called social sustainability. Generally defined as "a life-enhancing condition within communities, and a process within communities that can achieve that condition" (McKenzie, 2004). Social movements, civil society, and other formal and informal organisations can create institutional pressure on industry to abandon activities harmful to the environment.

Former studies reveal relations between environmental concerns and sustainable consumption behaviour (Saari et al., 2021). The COVID-19 pandemic is perceived as an accelerating factor for societal change (Sarkis et al., 2020) because implemented countermeasures have already proved to be effective, such as distant work and related digitalisation, shortening supply chains, exploiting the benefits of close distance inventories, and the possibilities for localised resources.

Changes in consumer behaviours are investigated as sufficiency being interpreted as reducing consumption levels mainly to reduce ecological footprints (Sandberg, 2021). Examples are absolute reductions, modal shifts, product longevity, and sharing practices (ibidem), which can be a core of business models. Scaling up and offering sustainable products as substitutions are the main activities associated with the strategic level at a large scale (Hernández-Chea et al., 2021).

Prior study about the transition towards a more specific sustainable business model, which is the circular business model, revealed six key conditions (Ćwiklicki

& O'Riordan, 2022). Those were regulations, societal culture, relationships with stakeholders, cooperation with consumers, management systems, and human, financial, and technological resources. They refer to all three levels where the business model operates. The main finding from investigating the success factors for transition was a contingency theory of transition to a CBM demonstrating that the transition depends on the characteristics of these conditions. It means that if the conditions support transitions, then a change is more probable. It explains why, in spite of internal organisational readiness to transform, the transition is not successful. Therefore, before making the decision to transition, an assessment of internal business capabilities supported by ecodesign tools, and also applied to the supply chain, should be performed.

References

Abdelkafi, N., & Täuscher, K. (2016). Business models for sustainability from a system dynamics perspective. *Organization and Environment*, *29*(1), 74–96. https://doi.org/10.1177/1086026615592930

Alcayaga, A., Wiener, M., & Hansen, E. G. (2019). Towards a framework of smart-circular systems: An integrative literature review. *Journal of Cleaner Production*, *221*, 622–634. https://doi.org/10.1016/j.jclepro.2019.02.085

Baldassarre, B., Calabretta, G., Bocken, N. M. P., & Jaskiewicz, T. (2017). Bridging sustainable business model innovation and user-driven innovation: A process for sustainable value proposition design. *Journal of Cleaner Production*, *147*, 175–186. https://doi.org/10.1016/j.jclepro.2017.01.081

Baldassarre, B., Keskin, D., Diehl, J. C., Bocken, N., & Calabretta, G. (2020). Implementing sustainable design theory in business practice: A call to action. *Journal of Cleaner Production*, *273*, 123113. https://doi.org/10.1016/j.jclepro.2020.123113

Bingham, C. B., & Davis, J. P. (2012). Learning sequences: Their existence, effect, and evolution. *Academy of Management Journal*, *55*(3), 611–641. https://doi.org/10.5465/amj.2009.0331

Bocken, N. M. P., Short, S. W., Rana, P., & Evans, S. (2014). A literature and practice review to develop sustainable business model archetypes. *Journal of Cleaner Production*, *65*, 42–56. https://doi.org/10.1016/j.jclepro.2013.11.039

Bocken, N., Short, S., Rana, P., & Evans, S. (2013). A value mapping tool for sustainable business modelling. *Corporate Governance: The International Journal of Business in Society*, *13*(5), 482–497. https://doi.org/10.1108/CG-06-2013-0078

Boons, F., & Lüdeke-Freund, F. (2013). Business models for sustainable innovation: State-of-the-art and steps towards a research agenda. *Journal of Cleaner Production*, *45*, 9–19. https://doi.org/10.1016/j.jclepro.2012.07.007

Bressanelli, G., Perona, M., & Saccani, N. (2017). Reshaping the washing machine industry through circular economy and product-service system business models. *64*, 43–48. https://doi.org/10.1016/j.procir.2017.03.065

Caldera, H. T. S., Desha, C., & Dawes, L. (2017). Exploring the role of lean thinking in sustainable business practice: A systematic literature review. *Journal of Cleaner Production*, *167*, 1546–1565. https://doi.org/10.1016/j.jclepro.2017.05.126

Ćwiklicki, M., & O'Riordan, L. (2017). Creating sustainable value: Sustainable development via new business models and reverse innovation. In *Sustainable business models: Principles, promise, and practice.*

Ćwiklicki, M., & O'Riordan, L. (2022). Enablers and barriers in the transition to Circular Business Models: Investigating the critical success factors for the tipping and break-even point. In M. Ćwiklicki, C. Ingrao & M. Wojnarowska (Eds.), *Sustainable products in the circular economy: Impact on business and society* (1st ed.). Routledge.

Doherty, B., Haugh, H., & Lyon, F. (2014). Social enterprises as hybrid organizations: A review and research agenda: Social enterprises as hybrid organizations. *International Journal of Management Reviews*, *16*(4), 417–436. https://doi.org/10.1111/ijmr.12028

Farla, J., Markard, J., Raven, R., & Coenen, L. (2012). Sustainability transitions in the making: A closer look at actors, strategies and resources. *Technological Forecasting and Social Change*, *79*(6), 991–998. https://doi.org/10.1016/j.techfore.2012.02.001

Ferlito, R., & Faraci, R. (2022). Business model innovation for sustainability: A new framework. *Innovation and Management Review*, *19*(3), 222–236. https://doi.org/10.1108/INMR-07-2021-0125

Geissdoerfer, M., Bocken, N. M. P., & Hultink, E. J. (2016). Design thinking to enhance the sustainable business modelling process—A workshop based on a value mapping process. *Journal of Cleaner Production*, *135*, 1218–1232. https://doi.org/10.1016/j.jclepro.2016.07.020

Geissdoerfer, M., Vladimirova, D., & Evans, S. (2018). Sustainable business model innovation: A review. *Journal of Cleaner Production*, *198*, 401–416. https://doi.org/10.1016/j.jclepro.2018.06.240

Gond, J.-P., El Akremi, A., Swaen, V., & Babu, N. (2017). The psychological microfoundations of corporate social responsibility: A person-centric systematic review: Micro-CSR: A systematic review. *Journal of Organizational Behavior*, *38*(2), 225–246. https://doi.org/10.1002/job.2170

Goni, F. A., Gholamzadeh Chofreh, A., Estaki Orakani, Z., Klemeš, J. J., Davoudi, M., & Mardani, A. (2021). Sustainable business model: A review and framework development. *Clean Technologies and Environmental Policy*, *23*(3), 889–897. https://doi.org/10.1007/s10098-020-01886-z

Govindan, K., Seuring, S., Zhu, Q., & Azevedo, S. G. (2016). Accelerating the transition towards sustainability dynamics into supply chain relationship management and governance structures. *Journal of Cleaner Production*, *112*, 1813–1823. https://doi.org/10.1016/j.jclepro.2015.11.084

Heikkurinen, P., Young, C. W., & Morgan, E. (2019). Business for sustainable change: Extending eco-efficiency and eco-sufficiency strategies to consumers. *Journal of Cleaner Production*, *218*, 656–664. https://doi.org/10.1016/j.jclepro.2019.02.053

Hernández-Chea, R., Jain, A., Bocken, N. M. P., & Gurtoo, A. (2021). The business model in sustainability transitions: A conceptualization. *Sustainability*, *13*(11), 5763. https://doi.org/10.3390/su13115763

Hobson, K. (2002). Competing discourses of sustainable consumption: Does the 'rationalisation of lifestyles' make sense? *Environmental Politics*, *11*(2), 95–120. https://doi.org/10.1080/714000601

Høgevold, N. M., & Svensson, G. (2012). A business sustainability model: A European case study. *Journal of Business and Industrial Marketing*, *27*(2), 142–151. https://doi.org/10.1108/08858621211197001

Hope, A. (2018). Sustainable business model design: A review of tools for developing responsible business models. In L. Moratis, F. Melissen, & S. O. Idowu (Eds.), *Sustainable business models* (pp. 377–394). Springer International Publishing. https://doi.org/10.1007/978-3-319-73503-0_17

ISO. (2020). *ISO 14006. Environmental management systems—Guidelines for incorporating ecodesign*. ISO.

Joyce, A., & Paquin, R. L. (2016). The triple layered business model canvas: A tool to design more sustainable business models. *Journal of Cleaner Production*, *135*, 1474–1486. https://doi.org/10.1016/j.jclepro.2016.06.067

Kazancoglu, Y., Ozkan-Ozen, Y. D., Sagnak, M., Kazancoglu, I., & Dora, M. (2023). Framework for a sustainable supply chain to overcome risks in transition to a circular economy through Industry 4.0. *Production Planning and Control*, *34*(10), 902–917. https://doi.org/10.1080/09537287.2021.1980910

Lozano, R. (2018). Sustainable business models: Providing a more holistic perspective. *Business Strategy and the Environment*, *27*(8), 1159–1166. https://doi.org/10.1002/bse.2059

Lüdeke-Freund, F., Bocken, N., Brent, A., & Musango, J. (2016). Business models for shared value: Main report. *Network for Business Sustainability south Afric*. https://www.researchgate.net/publication/311099469_Business_Models_for_Shared_Value_-_Main_Report

Malodia, S., & Bhatt, A. S. (2019). Why should I switch off: Understanding the barriers to sustainable consumption? *Vision: The Journal of Business Perspective*, *23*(2), 134–143. https://doi.org/10.1177/0972262919840197

McKenzie, S. (2004). Social sustainability: Towards some definitions (27; Hawke Research Institute Working Paper Series). University of South Australia. https://www.unisa.edu.au/siteassets/episerver-6-files/documents/eass/hri/working-papers/wp27.pdf

Morioka, S. N., Evans, S., & de Carvalho, M. M. (2016). Sustainable business model innovation: Exploring evidences in sustainability reporting. In G. Seliger, H. Kohl, & J. Mallon (Ed.), *13th global conference on sustainable manufacturing - Decoupling growth from resource use* (Vol. 40, pp. 659–667). https://doi.org/10.1016/j.procir.2016.01.151

Mura, M., Longo, M., Micheli, P., & Bolzani, D. (2018). The evolution of sustainability measurement research: The evolution of sustainability measurement research. *International Journal of Management Reviews*, *20*(3), 661–695. https://doi.org/10.1111/ijmr.12179

Niemann, J., Tichkiewitch, S., & Westkämper, E. (Eds.). (2009). *Design of sustainable product life cycles*. Springer.

O'Riordan, L. (2017). *Managing sustainable stakeholder relationships: Corporate approaches to responsible management* (1st ed.). Springer International Publishing. Imprint: Springer. https://doi.org/10.1007/978-3-319-50240-3

Osterwalder, A., & Pigneur, Y. (2010). *Business model generation: A handbook for visionaries, game changers, and challengers*. John Wiley & Sons.

Patala, S., Jalkala, A., Keränen, J., Väisänen, S., Tuominen, V., & Soukka, R. (2016). Sustainable value propositions: Framework and implications for technology suppliers. *Industrial Marketing Management*, *59*, 144–156. https://doi.org/10.1016/j.indmarman.2016.03.001

Pieroni, M. P. P., McAloone, T. C., & Pigosso, D. C. A. (2019). Business model innovation for circular economy and sustainability: A review of approaches. *Journal of Cleaner Production*, *215*, 198–216. https://doi.org/10.1016/j.jclepro.2019.01.036

Pilch, K., & Miśniakiewicz, M. (2022). Determinants of consumer behaviour – Towards sustainable consumption. In M. Ćwiklicki, C. Ingrao, & M. Wojnarowska (Eds.), *Sustainable products in the circular economy: Impact on business and society* (1st ed.). Routledge,220-245.

Porter, M. E., & Kramer, M. R. (2011). Creating shared value. *Harvard Business Review*, *89*(1), 62–77.

Reefke, H., & Sundaram, D. (2018). Sustainable supply chain management: Decision models for transformation and maturity. *Decision Support Systems*, *113*, 56–72. https://doi.org/10.1016/j.dss.2018.07.002

Roome, N., & Louche, C. (2016). Journeying toward business models for sustainability: A conceptual model found inside the black box of organisational transformation. *Organization and Environment*, *29*(1), 11–35. https://doi.org/10.1177/1086026615595084

Saari, U. A., Damberg, S., Frömbling, L., & Ringle, C. M. (2021). Sustainable consumption behavior of Europeans: The influence of environmental knowledge and risk perception on environmental concern and behavioral intention. *Ecological Economics*, *189*, 107155. https://doi.org/10.1016/j.ecolecon.2021.107155

Sandberg, M. (2021). Sufficiency transitions: A review of consumption changes for environmental sustainability. *Journal of Cleaner Production*, *293*, 126097. https://doi.org/10.1016/j.jclepro.2021.126097

Sarkis, J., Cohen, M. J., Dewick, P., & Schröder, P. (2020). A brave new world: Lessons from the COVID-19 pandemic for transitioning to sustainable supply and production. *Resources, Conservation and Recycling*, *159*, 104894. https://doi.org/10.1016/j.resconrec.2020.104894

Schaltegger, S., Hansen, E. G., & Lüdeke-Freund, F. (2016). Business models for sustainability: Origins, present research, and future avenues. *Organization and Environment*, *29*(1), 3–10. https://doi.org/10.1177/1086026615599806

Shakeel, J., Mardani, A., Chofreh, A. G., Goni, F. A., & Klemeš, J. J. (2020). Anatomy of sustainable business model innovation. *Journal of Cleaner Production*, *261*, 121201. https://doi.org/10.1016/j.jclepro.2020.121201

Shan, Y., Chin, T., & Mutsvene, N. (2023). The varying effects of four components of employee psychological capital on sustainable-business-model innovation in the new normal. *Sustainability*, *15*(15), 11787. https://doi.org/10.3390/su151511787

Smith, W. K., Gonin, M., & Besharov, M. L. (2013). Managing social-business tensions: A review and research agenda for social enterprise. *Business Ethics Quarterly*, *23*(3), 407–442. https://doi.org/10.5840/beq201323327

Stubbs, W., & Cocklin, C. (2008). Conceptualizing a "sustainability business model". *Organization and Environment*, *21*(2), 103–127. https://doi.org/10.1177/1086026608318042

Tao, J., & Yu, S. (2018). Product life cycle design for sustainable value creation: Methods of sustainable product development in the context of high value engineering. *Procedia CIRP*, *69*, 25–30. https://doi.org/10.1016/j.procir.2017.11.099

Unsworth, K. L., Davis, M. C., Russell, S. V., & Bretter, C. (2021). Employee green behaviour: How organizations can help the environment. *Current Opinion in Psychology*, *42*, 1–6. https://doi.org/10.1016/j.copsyc.2020.12.006

Urmanaviciene, A., & Praakli, M. (2021). Legal context and support incentives of social enterprises in Baltic countries. *Social Entrepreneurship Review*, *2*, 23–33. https://doi.org/10.15678/SER.2021.2.02

Vallet, F., Eynard, B., Millet, D., Mahut, S. G., Tyl, B., & Bertoluci, G. (2013). Using eco-design tools: An overview of experts' practices. *Design Studies*, *34*(3), 345–377. https://doi.org/10.1016/j.destud.2012.10.001

Vásquez, J., Aguirre, S., Puertas, E., Bruno, G., Priarone, P. C., & Settineri, L. (2021). A sustainability maturity model for micro, small and medium-sized enterprises (MSMEs) based on a data analytics evaluation approach. *Journal of Cleaner Production*, *311*, 127692. https://doi.org/10.1016/j.jclepro.2021.127692

Wojnarowska, M., Ćwiklicki, M., & Ingrao, C. (2022). *Sustainable products in the circular economy: Impact on business and society* (1st ed.). Routledge. https://doi.org/10.4324/9781003179788

Wojnarowska, M., Sołtysik, M., & Prusak, A. (2021). Impact of eco-labelling on the implementation of sustainable production and consumption. *Environmental Impact Assessment Review*, *86*, 106505. https://doi.org/10.1016/j.eiar.2020.106505

3 Sustainable product

3.1 Definition and scope of sustainable product

The significant cause of climate change is primarily attributed to the excessive exploitation of resources, which humanity has been practising since the Industrial Revolution of the 19th century (Eriksen, 2021). Global population growth has resulted in increased consumption and production in practically every aspect of life. Currently, resource consumption is equivalent to 1.7 Earths (Glavič, 2021). The realisation among people that not only war but also (paradoxically) peaceful, yet uncontrolled and unregulated, global development poses a serious threat to both our planet and its inhabitants has led to the rapid emergence of new economic models, including product policies, upon which the future existence of humanity depends (Rendtorff, 2019). The consequences of climate change are becoming increasingly noticeable, compelling decision-makers to adopt new ways of thinking about the economy (Yuille et al., 2021). As a result, in 2019, the European Green Deal was established as an action plan for a climate-neutral and economically competitive Europe, as presented in the document by the European Commission (2019).

In the past, environmental issues were often considered on a local scale, focusing primarily on the impacts associated with product life cycles. However, it is now widely recognised that these problems are far more intricate and encompass all stages of the life cycle, from material extraction to waste management (Berkhout & Smith, 1999). Historically, product design and manufacturing processes prioritised producing high-quality goods at minimal cost to enhance competitiveness (Bal & Erkan, 2019). While recycling and recovery were considered, they often had to compete solely on economic terms with the use of primary raw materials and disposal (Nowicki et al., 2023). Consequently, there is increasing pressure on industries in the 21st century to adopt more sustainable approaches to both product design and manufacturing (Baah et al., 2021). This pressure is further compounded by several factors, including the rising number and diversity of products, the creation of new product types through innovation, the global turnover of products, and the growing complexity of products. Manufacturing, according to Garg et al. (2015), accounts for nearly half of the world's total energy consumption, which has doubled over the past six decades (Garg, 2015). As a result, manufacturers face tremendous pressure to enhance competitiveness through increased productivity

DOI: 10.4324/9781032697895-4

while simultaneously delivering more sustainable products in response to heightened environmental awareness and responsibility (Javaid et al., 2022).

Previous research has predominantly focused on the concept of sustainable development in relation to ecological products that benefit the environment (Bhardwaj et al., 2020; Oláh et al., 2020; Sdrolia & Zarotiadis, 2019). Various definitions of green products exist, highlighting their aim to protect or enhance the environment by conserving energy and resources while reducing or eliminating the use of toxic substances, pollution, and waste (Diaz et al., 2021). Notably, research on the environmental impact of products has made significant strides in explaining how companies can develop greener products that contribute to their success, although this outcome is not always guaranteed (Hofenk et al., 2019).

While the focus on ecological products is essential, there is a need for further research to encompass a broader understanding of sustainability that incorporates social and economic aspects alongside the environmental dimension (Wojnarowska et al., 2022). This holistic approach recognises that sustainability extends beyond environmental considerations and includes the well-being of people and the long-term viability of businesses (Andersson et al., 2022). Integrating social and economic sustainability into product development strategies is vital for achieving comprehensive sustainable outcomes that benefit both society and the environment (Urbaniec et al., 2021).

Products have a significant impact on society throughout their life cycle, affecting various stakeholders such as employees, business owners, communities, and customers. It is crucial to optimise the impact of products not only on the environment but also on society, emphasising the need for sustainable rather than purely ecological products (Lin et al., 2019).

The development of sustainable products and services is increasingly recognised as an essential component of cleaner production and the circular economy (CE). The manufacturing industry faces growing legal, market, and financial pressures to create sustainable products in response to environmental policy and legislation (Mohammad Ebrahimi & Koh, 2021; Tavares-Lehmann & Varum, 2021). Initiatives such as Integrated Product Policy (IPP) and Extended Producer Responsibility further drive the demand for sustainable practices (Maxwell & van der Vorst, 2003).

Since 2001, the European Commission has been actively promoting IPP, which aims to support environmental product innovations and achieve broad reductions in all environmental impacts throughout a product's life cycle. This policy approach aligns with the emerging trend in environmentally advanced European countries, where a product-oriented environmental policy is gaining prominence (Murphy, 2001).

To achieve sustainable outcomes, it is crucial to utilise the Green Markets Policy Toolbox, focusing on both the demand (consumption) and supply (product development) sides (Buda & Ricz, 2023). This comprehensive approach recognises the need to address sustainability challenges at multiple levels and creates a balance among environmental, social, and economic considerations (Wojnarowska et al., 2022). By integrating sustainable practices into product development, companies can contribute to a more sustainable future while meeting evolving market demand and regulatory requirements (Sołtysik et al., 2019).

Research into the definition of sustainable products shows a lack of understanding of the fact that our planet itself is not a sustainable system. Only by adopting this assumption can a sustainable product be defined as a:

> product, which will give as little impact on the environment as possible during its life cycle. The life cycle in this simple definition includes extraction of raw material, production, use and final recycling (or deposition). The material in the product as well as the material (or element) used for producing energy is also included here. (Ljungberg, 2007)

Shuaib et al. define sustainable products through the prism of sustainable development as: "those that provide environmental, societal, and economic benefits while protecting public health, welfare, and the environment over their full commercial cycle" (Shuaib et al., 2014).

The concept of sustainable products involves a comprehensive approach that considers the economic, environmental, and social aspects of the triple bottom line (TBL) (Khan et al., 2023). The design and production of sustainable products require attention to all phases of the product life cycle. This holistic approach often requires the adoption of the 6Rs framework: reduction, reuse, recycling, recovery, redesign, and remanufacturing (Nowicki et al., 2023). These principles must be applied throughout the product life cycle to establish a circular material flow, where resources are utilised efficiently and waste is minimised (Shuaib et al., 2014).

To develop sustainable products, it is essential to consider economic factors, such as cost-effectiveness and long-term profitability (Alberti et al., 2000). Environmental considerations involve minimising resource consumption, reducing pollution and emissions, and ensuring responsible use and disposal of materials (Pimenov et al., 2022). Social aspects encompass factors like human rights, labour conditions, and community well-being (Ostrom, 2007). By addressing these three dimensions of sustainability in a comprehensive manner, companies can create products that align with the principles of the TBL and contribute to a more sustainable future (Fontaine & Rd, 2013; Khan et al., 2023).

Implementing the 6Rs throughout the product life cycle is key to achieving a circular material flow. Reduction involves minimising the use of resources and waste generation. Reuse entails extending the lifespan of products through repair, refurbishment, or repurposing (Wojnarowska et al., 2022). Recycling transforms waste materials into new resources. Recovery focuses on extracting value from waste through techniques like energy recovery. Redesign involves rethinking product design to optimise sustainability. Lastly, remanufacturing entails rebuilding products using reclaimed components. By adopting these principles, companies can promote resource efficiency, waste reduction, and a more sustainable approach to product development and consumption (Nowicki et al., 2023; Potting et al., 2017).

According to Ljungberg (2007), developing sustainable products involves following certain guidelines, including reducing material and energy consumption throughout the product's service life, minimising emissions, dispersion, and toxin formation throughout the product life cycle, increasing the use of recyclable materials, utilising renewable resources for production, extending the product's service life, minimising environmental impact at every stage of the life cycle, substituting products with services, implementing "reverse logistics", enhancing product performance during use, selecting materials with low environmental pollution, limiting the use of rare materials, choosing clean materials for production processes, avoiding the generation of hazardous and toxic materials, and utilising materials with low energy consumption (Ljungberg, 2007). These rules serve as a framework for creating products that are environmentally responsible and contribute to sustainable development.

Meeting all sustainability demands throughout the entire life cycle of a product is a highly challenging task. As a result, different types of sustainable products tend to prioritise different aspects at various stages of the life cycle (Anex & Lifset, 2014). A sustainable product is generally understood as one that addresses the challenges of sustainable development by delivering ecological, economic, and social benefits while safeguarding public health, well-being, and the environment across the entire life cycle (Diaz et al., 2021; Fargnoli et al., 2014). It can be seen as an ideal, a form of excellence that manufacturers constantly strive for, continuously improving specific aspects of the product (Sanyé-Mengual et al., 2014). Achieving complete sustainability throughout the product's life cycle remains an ongoing process, as manufacturers work towards enhancing different dimensions of sustainability and advancing towards the ideal of a truly sustainable product.

When evaluating the sustainability of products, it is essential to consider not only their environmental impact but also the socioeconomic aspects associated with their production, use, and disposal (Sanyé-Mengual et al., 2014). Assessing the entire life cycle of a product provides a holistic view of its sustainability performance and ensures that all stages, from raw material extraction to end-of-life management, are taken into account (Deschamps et al., 2018).

In order to establish clear criteria and standards for sustainable products, certification systems and accompanying signs play a vital role (Varese et al., 2022). These systems provide a rigorous and independent assessment process that examines various dimensions of sustainability (Wojnarowska et al., 2021). They consider both ecological and social factors, ensuring that products meet specific criteria related to environmental impact, resource efficiency, social responsibility, and ethical practices (Kabaja et al., 2022).

Certification systems cover a wide range of aspects, including raw material sourcing, energy and water usage during manufacturing, waste generation, product durability, recyclability, labour conditions, fair trade practices, and social equity (Nowicki et al., 2021). They are designed to ensure that sustainable products adhere to high standards and are verified by independent institutions to maintain credibility and transparency (Varese et al., 2022).

By relying on these certification systems, consumers, businesses, and other stakeholders can make informed choices and support sustainable practices. The presence of certification labels on products provides a tangible and recognisable symbol of their sustainability credentials. It helps consumers identify products that align with their values and encourages businesses to adopt more sustainable production processes and supply chains (Schumacher, 2010). Moreover, certification systems contribute to raising awareness about sustainability issues and driving market demand for sustainable products. They incentivise companies to improve their environmental and social performance, foster innovation in sustainable design and production, and promote a shift towards a more sustainable economy (Thøgersen et al., 2010). Overall, certification systems and accompanying signs play a crucial role in defining and promoting sustainable products. They ensure that sustainability criteria are met throughout the entire life cycle of products, encompassing both ecological and social considerations. By establishing clear standards and providing independent verification, these systems facilitate the transition towards more sustainable consumption and production patterns (Gordy, 2003).

3.2 Unleashing the power of the circular economy: Driving sustainable product transformation

It is worth emphasising that the economy of the past 150 years has been built on a linear model (take, make, use, and dispose), characterised by resource extraction for production and consumption, with no plans for waste reutilisation or active regeneration of the economy (Romer, 1994). The accepted linear model of the economy, over time, has been recognised as the root cause of numerous issues primarily associated with the following factors: the extraction of virgin materials at a rate exceeding their natural replenishment capacity; the disposal of post-use products in landfills or incineration plants, resulting in the loss of valuable and scarce resources, which are then newly extracted to manufacture new goods; the unsafe handling of waste in the linear economy, leading to the leaching of hazardous substances into soil, water, and air, thus causing alarming environmental pollution; and the significant energy consumption and environmental pollution resulting from both product manufacturing and transportation. Consequently, linear economies can be regarded as completely unsustainable from environmental, economic, and social perspectives (Korhonen et al., 2018).

In the given context, the concept of CE offers a promising alternative that focuses on maximising the usefulness and value of products, components, and materials (Corona et al., 2019). It presents itself as a sustainable economic model that aims to break the traditional link between economic growth and the depletion of resources (D'Amato et al., 2017).

In the CE framework, products and materials are treated as valuable resources, even after their initial purpose has been fulfilled. Instead of being discarded, these items are redirected into a closed-loop system, where they serve as zero-burden resources. Through various strategies like recycling, refurbishing, remanufacturing, and upcycling, the materials are transformed into secondary raw materials, which can then be used as inputs in the production of new goods with added value (Saidani et al., 2017). By promoting the continuous circulation and reuse of materials, the CE minimises waste generation and reduces reliance on extracting new resources. This approach not only contributes to resource conservation and environmental protection but also fosters economic growth and innovation by creating new business opportunities and value chains centred around resource efficiency (Gall et al., 2020). In essence, it strives to create a regenerative system where resources are utilised in a more sustainable and responsible manner, ensuring their long-term availability while minimising their negative impacts on the environment and society (Moreno et al., 2016).

The CE is recognised as a crucial driver for achieving sustainable development in industrial economics. It offers a unique approach that harmonises the goals of economic growth and environmental protection, standing in opposition to the conventional linear model that has significant negative impacts (Korhonen et al., 2018).

According to Ghisellini et al. (2016), it provides a reliable framework that brings about a fundamental transformation in the existing business model. This transformation focuses on the adoption of preventive and regenerative eco-industrial development systems, with the ultimate aim of improving overall well-being through the restoration of environmental integrity (Ghisellini et al., 2016).

In essence, the CE not only seeks to create a more sustainable and resilient industrial system but also emphasises the importance of recovering and preserving the environment as a means to enhance societal well-being. By shifting towards a circular approach, businesses can mitigate their environmental footprint, reduce resource depletion, and promote the restoration of ecological systems, leading to a more prosperous and balanced future (Cwiklicki & Wojnarowska, 2020).

According to Moraga et al. (2019), this approach stands apart from the linear economy due to its core principles of slowing and closing resource loops. These two features are not mutually exclusive but rather complementary. Slowing refers to the design of long-lasting goods and solutions that extend or intensify the utilisation time of products, thus reducing the pace of resource consumption. On the other hand, closing involves the integration of a closed loop between the end-of-life stage and production, where post-use products are recirculated as zero-burden resources within the life cycle to generate secondary raw materials (Moraga et al., 2019).

In this context, the CE can be understood through seven interconnected patterns of production and consumption, which, when combined, reinforce each other and contribute to its overall effectiveness (Korhonen et al., 2018; Wijkman & Skånberg, 2015):

- sustainable procurement involves the development and implementation of responsible purchasing policies to ensure that products and services are sourced in an environmentally and socially responsible manner.
- ecodesign focuses on designing products and services in a way that minimises their environmental impact throughout their entire life cycle.
- industrial and territorial ecology explores opportunities for eco-industrial synergies within specific business areas. This approach encourages companies to

view waste as a resource that can be utilised by others, creating value-added commodities and minimising waste generation.

- the economics of functionality promote a collaborative economy that prioritises the use of products over ownership. Instead of selling products themselves, companies offer services related to the products, fostering a more sustainable and efficient use of resources.
- responsible consumption aims to encourage rational consumption patterns and the selection of products based on social and ecological criteria. This approach empowers consumers to make informed choices that align with sustainability goals.
- extending the lifespan of products is achieved through repair, reuse, and repurposing. By keeping products in use for longer periods, resource consumption and waste generation can be significantly reduced.
- recycling involves transforming collected waste materials into secondary raw materials through a controlled process. The creation of a market for these recycled materials is essential to ensure their successful integration into the CE.

By implementing and integrating these patterns, the circular approach can create a more sustainable and regenerative system where resources are used efficiently, waste is minimised, and economic growth is decoupled from resource depletion (Ellen MacArthur Foundation, 2012).

The successful transition to a circular model of the economy requires active involvement and commitment of all key stakeholders involved in the life cycle of products. These stakeholders include producers and consumers/users, as well as decision-makers and policymakers (McDowall et al., 2017). Achieving this goal relies on value co-creation among these actors, recognising their shared responsibility in driving the viability of the circular approach. Importantly, such collaboration can have far-reaching positive impacts on various aspects of society, including the social fabric of communities, the economic sufficiency of regions, and the overall safety, integrity, and quality of the natural environment (Prieto-Sandoval et al., 2018).

By embracing a holistic and integrated approach, the CE can significantly contribute to the three dimensions of sustainability: environmental, economic, and social. This comprehensive perspective ensures that the environmental impact is minimised, economic systems become more resilient and resource-efficient, and social well-being is enhanced. The circular model prioritises long-term thinking and considers the well-being of both present and future generations, acknowledging the interconnectedness of ecological, economic, and social systems. Through its integrative approach, the CE offers a promising pathway to address the complex challenges of our time and build a more sustainable and prosperous future for all (Corona et al., 2019).

The emergence and growth of the CE are driven by the recognition that the Earth operates as a closed and finite system, with limited resources and a limited capacity to tolerate environmental degradation. It is crucial for the economy and the environment to coexist in order to preserve the Earth's carrying capacity (Hysa et al., 2020). To achieve this, sustainability-oriented strategies, such as those outlined in the CE Action Plan (European Commission, 2015a), need to be adopted. The European Union has been actively working on the transition to a carbon-neutral and circular economy through the implementation and dissemination of this comprehensive set of actions (European Commission, 2015a, 2015b). Global organisations such as OECD, WEF, and UNEP actively advocate for the closure of material loops through various reports and events (OECD, 2016; UNEP, 2011; WEF, 2016).

The adoption of a circular approach to products holds significant potential for sustainability in its broadest sense, with benefits for people, the planet, and prosperity. A sustainable CE focuses on designing and promoting products that are durable, reusable, repairable, and remanufacturable, rather than simply recovering their material or energy content and constantly producing new items (Polverini, 2021). This prioritisation of extending the functional value of products is integral to circular models. The approach emphasises reuse, repair, and recycling, thereby reducing waste and promoting sustainable practices in manufacturing and consumption (Luttropp & Lagerstedt, 2006). Furthermore, it contributes to energy conservation and helps prevent irreversible environmental damage caused by the excessive extraction and utilisation of resources, which surpasses the Earth's capacity to renew them (Pimenov et al., 2022).

Durable products have a long lifespan and can be repaired multiple times when they break. When consumers no longer need these products, they can be passed on or sold to other consumers for reuse (Young et al., 2010). Alternatively, if reuse is not possible, their materials can be recycled with minimal remaining resources going to energy recovery (Domenech & Bahn-Walkowiak, 2019). In an ecodesign-based CE, consumable products like food, drinks, cosmetics, and detergents should be produced with minimal resource impact and generate minimal waste. Actions should also be taken to minimise emissions and climate impacts throughout the entire product life cycle. Implementing these practices would result in reduced resource usage, waste, and emissions, while creating more jobs in repair and recycling sectors and leading to cost savings, all while preserving the functionality of products (Pigosso et al., 2017).

Given the potential of the CE to enhance the sustainability of products and services throughout their life cycle, it has garnered significant attention from researchers, decision-makers, policymakers, and managers (Hysa et al., 2020).

In order to achieve sustainable development, it is crucial to integrate ecological and economic considerations into decision-making processes. This integration should occur at all levels of institutions, from government policies to businesses and households. Balancing economic goals with environmental and social objectives poses a significant challenge for producers, consumers, governments, social organisations, and other economic actors (Buhl et al., 2019).

Enterprises are particularly impacted by environmental protection requirements, which are often governed by legal regulations (Sołtysik et al., 2019). While these regulations are aimed at safeguarding the environment, they can be perceived by businesses as additional costs. Enterprises need to budget for the increasing expenses associated with environmental compliance and invest in environmental protection measures. Consequently, modern company management should view environmental protection as an integral part of the overall management process (Urbaniec et al., 2021).

To address these challenges, a shift from the current linear model of the economy to a sustainable CE is necessary. The objective is to achieve the highest possible levels of waste recovery, recycling, and proper management within the production cycle. This transition requires fulfilling specific conditions and promoting policies that prioritise the use of renewable resources and natural processes (Korhonen et al., 2018). A crucial objective is to develop environmentally friendly products and services that prioritise safety for the environment. Achieving this goal involves integrating ecological considerations into the product design phase. Designing products with ecological features is vital as it enables the transfer of waste materials with specific properties back into the production process or their utilisation by other entities (Diaz et al., 2021). By incorporating ecological principles from the outset, product designers can minimise environmental impacts and optimise resource utilisation. This approach, known as ecodesign or green design, aims to create products that are environmentally responsible throughout their entire life cycle. Ecodesign involves considering factors such as material selection, energy efficiency, waste reduction, recyclability, and the overall environmental footprint of the product (Braungart et al., 2007; Ljungberg, 2007). To facilitate the transfer of waste materials back into the production process, the concept of a closed-loop system is crucial. This approach emphasises the recovery and recycling of waste materials, transforming them into valuable resources.

Design principles known as xR are at the core of circular development, capturing the essence of the CE approach (Geissdoerfer et al., 2017; Ghisellini et al., 2016). These principles are often referred to in literature as R-hierarchies or R-imperatives, highlighting the importance of prioritising actions that align with the principles of CE (Reike et al., 2018).

Already in the 1990s, several key researchers in industrial ecology defined a hierarchy of resource retention, identifying three to five stages (Ayres & Ayres, 1996). Although xR was initiated by the 3Rs (reduce, reuse, recycle) as the accepted concept of CE in theory and practice, recent emphasis has been placed on more nuanced hierarchies. Authors not only propose different numbers of R-imperatives, such as 3R, 4R, or 6R, but also confer them different attributes and meanings (Badurdeen et al., 2009). This situation has led to various conceptualisations of xR in the literature. Expanded beyond the production sphere, the 3R concept now includes changes in the behaviour of consumers, who have been familiarised with excessive consumption and improper product disposal, often resulting in premature waste generation instead of proper management. The ultimate consequences of the R strategy for a finished product are therefore the result of a sequence of decision-making steps involving different actors (Abdel-Shafy & Mansour, 2018).

Currently, the number of distinguished xR imperatives ranges from 3R to 10R (Potting et al., 2017). An advanced strategy utilising ten R-based approaches, such as refuse, rethink, reduce, reuse, repair, refurbish, remanufacture, repurpose, recycle, and recover, can contribute to achieving cleaner production and help companies gain a competitive advantage (Bag et al., 2021; Kirchherr et al.,

2017). According to Lagerstedt and Luttropp, xR combines the waste priorities of the European Union with the ten principles of ecodesign in practice (Luttropp & Lagerstedt, 2006).

Diaz et al. (2021) note that the discourse on preserving the value of products primarily revolves around the widely used terminology of the 3Rs (reduce, reuse, recycle), sometimes supplemented by the concept of recovering materials (4Rs). Reike et al.'s (2018) research supports this observation, indicating that the 3R typology is most prevalent in the literature. However, it is worth noting that the waste management and environmental sciences field tends to emphasise the 5R framework, while discussions in reverse logistics and closed-loop supply chain management often encompass the 4R, 5R, and 6R strategies. Less common in the literature are the more detailed typologies, such as the 7Rs–10Rs, which highlight a significant research gap that remains to be addressed (Nowicki et al., 2023).

There is a growing recognition of new phenomena in the realm of consumption, which requires not only governmental efforts but also active involvement from other market participants, including consumers. Promoting environmental protection becomes a shared responsibility, emphasising the importance of fostering environmental awareness and cultivating a modern perception of effective economic processes rooted in ethical and ecological principles (Alamsyah & Febriani, 2020; Rosli & Ahmad, 2019). In order to establish a functional CE model, reliable knowledge derived from the heightened environmental consciousness of all market participants is crucial. One of the key challenges lies in developing a system that educates consumers about the environmental impact of products throughout their life cycle, while providing producers with the opportunity to communicate the benefits of their offers. Eco-labelling emerges as a prominent solution and is considered a vital tool for consumer education regarding environmentally friendly products (Bertrandias et al., 2017). Purchasing organic products, for instance, offers tangible benefits by reducing humanity's negative environmental impact and aligning with the overarching objectives of sustainable production and consumption. However, achieving these goals relies on heightened environmental awareness among consumers (Varese et al., 2023; Varese et al., 2022). Therefore, environmental education becomes a critical means of communication and information, enabling consumers to consciously interpret eco-labels and make informed product choices based on them (Kabaja et al., 2022; Wojnarowska et al., 2021). Failure to meet this condition may result in information overload from advertising and marketing campaigns, leading to the misinterpretation of messages by the target audience. For eco-labelling to have a positive effect, it must be scientifically standardised, and consumer environmental awareness must be elevated (Chen & Chang, 2013).

Another crucial aspect is the successful implementation of a strategy for transitioning from conventional products to sustainable alternatives. A fundamental component of this strategy is setting the right pricing for sustainable products. Customers are more likely to be interested in these products if they experience direct financial benefits (Chekima et al., 2016). Preferential pricing can be achieved through measures like differentiated taxation, such as applying a reduced VAT rate to biodegradable products. Thus, it becomes essential to create and support markets for environmentally friendly products by implementing policies that encourage preferential pricing, employing a robust environmental labelling system, and establishing effective standardisation processes (Riskos et al., 2021).

3.3 Sustainable product design

The literature extensively explores the concept of ecodesign from diverse perspectives and disciplines, providing a comprehensive understanding of this approach. Various authors offer distinct definitions of ecodesign, contributing to a rich and multifaceted discourse. Baumann et al. (2002) emphasise ecodesign as a holistic approach that encompasses the identification of environmental issues and their underlying causes. It involves exerting influence over the entire life cycle of material goods, from conception and production to use, reuse, recycling, and final disposal (Baumann et al., 2002). Deutz et al. (2013) view ecodesign as the integration of environmental criteria into product design, aiming to minimise environmental impacts across all stages of the life cycle. They highlight the need to consider environmental factors in the design and development process to achieve sustainable outcomes (Deutz et al., 2013).

Due to the absence of a universally accepted definition, the literature explores the concept of ecodesign in relation to various aspects. Researchers analyse the environmental and social implications of ecodesign, recognising its potential to minimise the environmental burden of products throughout their life cycle. In the literature, numerous examples of ecodesign initiatives can also be found, focusing on particular products such as electronic products (Yung et al., 2012) or the creation of ecodesign tools, with a specific case being Negny et al.'s study (2012), which investigates ecodesign in the chemical industry (Negny et al., 2012). Maccioni et al. (2019) delve into different industries and examine the impact of ecodesign on reducing environmental impacts (Maccioni et al., 2019). Through these analyses, researchers aim to enhance our understanding of ecodesign's influence on sustainability across diverse sectors.

The social aspect of ecodesign has been a significant focus of research by several authors, including Paparoidamis et al. (2019), and Zeng et al. (2020), who conducted studies to assess the knowledge level, needs, and expectations related to eco-innovation (Paparoidamis et al., 2019; Zeng et al., 2021). Komeijani et al. (2016) developed guidelines aimed at designing products that encourage environmentally sustainable consumer behaviour (Komeijani et al., 2016).

To address the social aspects of ecodesign, the sustainable behaviour design (SBD) framework has been introduced. This framework integrates various design concepts such as ergonomics, emotional design, preventive design, and interaction design, aligning them with fundamental consumer needs. The goal is to increase awareness among consumers about their behaviours and decision-making processes, promoting reflective thinking and fostering sustainable behaviours, even in cases where users may not be consciously aware (automatic thinking) (Kim & Chung, 2018).

Paparoidamis et al. (2019) conducted research that identified existing barriers to the purchase of environmentally friendly products. They proposed potential strategies and measures to overcome these barriers. The study conducted by Maccioni et al. (2019) provided valuable insights into consumer responses to eco-innovative product projects across various industries. These findings contribute to a better understanding of consumer behaviour and can inform the development of effective ecodesign strategies.

Another research area in the literature focuses on the use of ecodesign methods and tools to assess the environmental impact of products throughout their life cycle. La Pochat et al. (2007) categorised and described seven key tool groups, including life cycle assessment (LCA), simplified LCA, eco-matrix, Checklist, Ecoparametric tool, Guidelines, and Manual. They also developed the ecodesign integration method (EDIMS) to facilitate ecodesign implementation in businesses (Le Pochat et al., 2007).

Byggeth and Hochschorner (2006) compared various methods such as ABC-analysis, the environmentally responsible product assessment matrix (ERPA), MECO, MET-Matrix, Philips Fast Five Awareness, Funktionkosten, Dominance Matrix, Paired Comparison, EcoDesign Checklist, Econcept Spiderweb, environmental objectives deployment (EOD), LiDS-wheel, The Morphological Box, and Prescribing tools Strat. These studies assessed the usefulness of these tools for evaluating environmental impacts (Byggeth & Hochschorner, 2006).

Cholewa-Wójcik and Kawecka (2022) conducted an interesting review of sustainable product design tools. The authors indicated that, for example, Yi et al. (2020) proposed an energy characteristic evaluation tool as an alternative to LCA. This tool incorporates simulation tools for energy consumption forecasting, energy performance evaluation models, and overall workflow analysis. Yokokawa et al. (2020) developed product design tools like life cycle asset management (LCAM) and function network diagram (FND), which integrate functional and environmental aspects throughout the product's life cycle. Molina-Besch and Pålsson (2020) presented an interesting tool, the environmental evaluation tool for food packaging (EEFP), which supports ecodesign in the food industry and does not require expert knowledge for utilisation. Additionally, no significant differences were found in the results compared with LCA. Furthermore, software tools are highlighted by many authors and can be categorised as autonomous or integrated with CAD systems. These programmes are considered crucial for supporting ecodesign efforts (Cholewa-Wójcik & Kawecka, 2022; Molina-Morales & Martínez-Fernández, 2010; Yi et al., 2020; Yokokawa et al., 2020).

It is important to note that different market entities, including manufacturers, consumers, and recyclers, have varying perspectives on ecodesign. Their approaches to design, considering products within a closed-loop economy, may lack consistency due to their differing interests.

Ecodesign plays a crucial role in the transition to a CE for businesses (Cholewa-Wojcik et al., 2023). It involves complying with legal requirements and considering the economic viability of solutions, while also benefiting company development through innovative technologies. Competitiveness is important, but some companies prioritise short-term gains, hindering positive market transformations (Dahmani et al., 2022). From a consumer perspective, ecodesign aims to provide socially friendly, functional products with extended lifespans and affordable options. Consumers value informative product labelling that highlights ecological characteristics, proper use, and waste management practices (Kabaja et al., 2022). Establishing a unified and consumer-friendly labelling system requires industry collaboration to involve consumers in closing the loop. Raising consumer awareness is essential for successful ecodesign implementation (MacDonald & She, 2015).

Recyclers face specific challenges and considerations in implementing ecodesign practices. One significant criterion for recyclers is ensuring compliance with legal requirements related to ecodesign, which are shaped by market practices and advancements in technology. Adhering to these regulations is essential for recyclers to effectively integrate ecodesigned products into the CE. Obtaining high-quality waste materials and ensuring easy processing of raw materials present ongoing challenges for recyclers. Ecodesigned products should be designed in a way that facilitates the extraction of valuable materials and minimises difficulties in the recycling process. This requires careful consideration of product design and material choices to optimise recyclability (Cholewa-Wojcik et al., 2023).

Moreover, ecodesign has a direct impact on the required recycling technologies. Recyclers need to adapt and develop their processes to efficiently handle ecodesigned products, which may have unique material compositions and structures. This includes investing in appropriate sorting, separation, and processing technologies to effectively recover valuable resources from these products. To address these challenges, ecodesign must be approached holistically, considering the interests of all stakeholders involved. Designing products in line with ecodesign principles involves considering the entire life cycle, from production to end-of-life management (Maris et al., 2014). This includes designing products for extended use and incorporating principles of durability, repairability, and upgradability. Assessing the economic feasibility of ecodesign is also crucial, ensuring that the production and sale of ecodesigned products are profitable while remaining affordable for consumers.

The practical availability and convenience of ecodesign solutions play a significant role in their adoption by both manufacturers and consumers. Implementing ecodesign measures should not introduce unnecessary complexity or compromise user experience. Additionally, designing products with easily separable and combinable modules promotes modularity, allowing for efficient disassembly and recycling while maintaining product integrity (Cholewa-Wójcik & Kawecka, 2022; Wojnarowska & Salerno-Kochan, 2022).

Furthermore, effective communication is essential to raise awareness and promote the adoption of ecodesigned products. Educating consumers about the benefits of ecodesign, including extended product lifecycles and responsible waste management, encourages their active participation in the CE. Introducing new forms of ownership and innovative business models that align with ecodesign principles can further drive consumer engagement and adoption (Kabaja et al., 2022; Varese et al., 2022).

In summary, ecodesign plays a crucial role in transitioning the economy towards sustainable products. It requires considering the entire life cycle of a product, from production to end-of-life management. Implementing ecodesign necessitates collaboration among all stakeholders and a comprehensive approach that addresses economic, social, and environmental aspects.

References

Abdel-Shafy, H. I., & Mansour, M. S. M. (2018). Solid waste issue: Sources, composition, disposal, recycling, and valorization. In *Egyptian Journal of Petroleum* (Vol. 27, Issue 4, pp. 1275–1290). Egyptian Petroleum Research Institute. https://doi.org/10.1016/j.ejpe.2018.07.003

Alamsyah, D. P., & Febriani, R. (2020). Green customer behaviour: Impact of green brand awareness to green trust. *Journal of Physics: Conference Series*, *1477*(7), 072022. https://doi.org/10.1088/1742-6596/1477/7/072022

Alberti, M., Caini, L., Calabrese, A., & Rossi, D. (2000). Evaluation of the costs and benefits of an environmental management system. *International Journal of Production Research*, *38*(17), 4455–4466. https://doi.org/10.1080/00207540050205226

Andersson, S., Svensson, G., Molina-Castillo, F., Otero-Neira, C., Lindgren, J., Karlsson, N. P. E., & Laurell, H. (2022). Sustainable development—Direct and indirect effects between economic, social, and environmental dimensions in business practices. *Corporate Social Responsibility and Environmental Management*, *29*(5), 1158–1172. https://doi.org/10.1002/csr.2261

Anex, R., & Lifset, R. (2014). Life cycle assessment – A guide to approaches, experiences and information sources. *Journal of Industrial Ecology*, Yale University, 18(3), 321-323.

Ayres, R. U., & Ayres, W. L. (1996). *Industrial ecology*. Edward Elgar Publishing Limited.

Baah, C., Opoku-Agyeman, D., Acquah, I. S. K., Agyabeng-Mensah, Y., Afum, E., Faibil, D., & Abdoulaye, F. A. M. (2021). Examining the correlations between stakeholder pressures, green production practices, firm reputation, environmental and financial performance: Evidence from manufacturing SMEs. *Sustainable Production and Consumption*, *27*, 100–114. https://doi.org/10.1016/j.spc.2020.10.015

Badurdeen, F., Iyengar, D., Goldsby, T. J., Metta, H., Gupta, S., & Jawahir, I. S. (2009). Extending total life-cycle thinking to sustainable supply chain design. *International Journal of Product Lifecycle Management*, *4*(1/2/3), 49. https://doi.org/10.1504/IJPLM.2009.031666

Bag, S., Gupta, S., & Kumar, S. (2021). Industry 4.0 adoption and 10R advance manufacturing capabilities for sustainable development. *International Journal of Production Economics*, *231*, 107844. https://doi.org/10.1016/j.ijpe.2020.107844

Bal, H. Ç., & Erkan, Ç. (2019). Industry 4.0 and competitiveness. *Procedia Computer Science*, *158*, 625–631. https://doi.org/10.1016/j.procs.2019.09.096

Baumann, H., Boons, F., & Bragd, A. (2002). Mapping the green product development field: Engineering, policy and business perspectives. *Journal of Cleaner Production*, *10*(5), 409–425. https://doi.org/10.1016/S0959-6526(02)00015-X

Berkhout, F., & Smith, D. (1999). Products and the environment: An integrated approach to policy. *European Environment*, *9*(5), 174–185. https://doi.org/10.1002/(SICI)1099-0976(199909/10)9:5<174::AID-EET204>3.0.CO;2-6

Bertrandias, L., Bernard, Y., Bertrandias, L., & Bernard, Y. (2017). The environmental labelling rollout of consumer goods by public authorities: Analysis of and lessons learned from the French case. *Journal of Cleaner Production*, *161*, 688–697. https://doi.org/10.1016/j.jclepro.2017.05.179

Bhardwaj, A. K., Garg, A., Ram, S., Gajpal, Y., & Zheng, C. (2020). Research trends in green product for environment: A bibliometric perspective. *International Journal of Environmental Research and Public Health*. https://doi.org/10.3390/ijerph17228469

Braungart, M., McDonough, W., & Bollinger, A. (2007). Cradle-to-cradle design: Creating healthy emissions - A strategy for eco-effective product and system design. *Journal of Cleaner Production*. https://doi.org/10.1016/j.jclepro.2006.08.003

Buda, G., & Ricz, J. (2023). Industrial symbiosis and industrial policy for sustainable development in Uganda. *Review of Evolutionary Political Economy*, *4*(1), 165–189. https://doi.org/10.1007/s43253-023-00097-8

Buhl, A., Schmidt-keilich, M., Muster, V., Blazejewski, S., Schrader, U., Harrach, C., & Sch, M. (2019). Design thinking for sustainability : Why and how design thinking can foster sustainability-oriented innovation development. *Journal of Cleaner Production*, *231*, 1248–1257. https://doi.org/10.1016/j.jclepro.2019.05.259

Byggeth, S., & Hochschorner, E. (2006). Handling trade-offs in ecodesign tools for sustainable product development and procurement. *Journal of Cleaner Production*, *14*(15–16), 1420–1430. https://doi.org/10.1016/j.jclepro.2005.03.024

Chekima, B., Wafa, S. K. S. A. W., Igau, O. A., Chekima, S., & Sondoh, S. L. (2016). Examining green consumerism motivational drivers: Does premium price and demographics matter to green purchasing? *Journal of Cleaner Production*, *112*, 3436–3450. https://doi.org/10.1016/j.jclepro.2015.09.102

Chen, Y.-S., & Chang, C.-H. (2013). Greenwash and green trust: The mediation effects of green consumer confusion and green perceived risk. *Journal of Business Ethics*, *114*(3), 489–500. https://doi.org/10.1007/s10551-012-1360-0

Cholewa-Wojcik, A., Cwiklicki, M., Kawecka, A., & Wojnarowska, M. (2023). Identification of the expectations of selected entities in the supply chain regarding the properties of the designed food packaging. *International Journal for Quality Research*, *17*(2), 341–358. https://doi.org/10.24874/IJQR17.02-03

Cholewa-Wójcik, A., & Kawecka, A. (2022). Challenges of eco-design of integrated products. In *Sustainable products in the circular economy* (pp. 18–35). Routledge. https://doi.org/10.4324/9781003179788-2

Corona, B., Shen, L., Reike, D., Rosales Carreón, J., & Worrell, E. (2019). Towards sustainable development through the circular economy—A review and critical assessment on current circularity metrics. *Resources, Conservation and Recycling*, *151*, 104498. https://doi.org/10.1016/j.resconrec.2019.104498

Fontaine, M., & Rd, W. (2013). Corporate social responsibility and sustainability : The new bottom line ? *National Louis University*, *4*(4), 110–119.

Cwiklicki, M., & Wojnarowska, M. (2020). Circular economy and industry 4.0: One-way or two-way relationships? *Engineering Economics*, *31*(4). https://doi.org/10.5755/j01.ee.31.4.24565

D'Amato, D., Droste, N., Allen, B., Kettunen, M., Lähtinen, K., Korhonen, J., … Toppinen, A. (2017). Green, circular, bio economy: A comparative analysis of sustainability avenues. *Journal of Cleaner Production*. https://doi.org/10.1016/j.jclepro.2017.09.053

Dahmani, N., Belhadi, A., Benhida, K., Elfezazi, S., Touriki, F. E., & Azougagh, Y. (2022). Integrating lean design and eco-design to improve product design: From literature review to an operational framework. *Energy and Environment*, *33*(1), 189–219. https://doi.org/10.1177/0958305X21993481

Deschamps, J., Simon, B., Tagnit-Hamou, A., & Amor, B. (2018). Is open-loop recycling the lowest preference in a circular economy? Answering through LCA of glass powder in concrete. *Journal of Cleaner Production*. https://doi.org/10.1016/j.jclepro.2018.03.021

Deutz, P., McGuire, M., & Neighbour, G. (2013). Eco-design practice in the context of a structured design process: An interdisciplinary empirical study of UK manufacturers. *Journal of Cleaner Production*, *39*, 117–128. https://doi.org/10.1016/j.jclepro.2012.08.035

Diaz, A., Schöggl, J.-P., Reyes, T., & Baumgartner, R. J. (2021). Sustainable product development in a circular economy: Implications for products, actors, decision-making support and lifecycle information management. *Sustainable Production and Consumption*, *26*, 1031–1045. https://doi.org/10.1016/j.spc.2020.12.044

Domenech, T., & Bahn-Walkowiak, B. (2019). Transition towards a resource efficient circular economy in Europe: Policy lessons from the EU and the member states. *Ecological Economics*. https://doi.org/10.1016/j.ecolecon.2017.11.001

Ellen MacArthur Foundation. (2012). Ellen Mcarthur towards a circular economy. *Journal of Industrial Ecology*. https://doi.org/10.1162/108819806775545321

Erica, V., Chiara, C. M., Luigi, B., Bartłomiej, K., & Magdalena, W. (2022). Consumers' perception towards quality certifications : Is this the key to help rural areas' resilience? *Economic Growth in the Conditions of Globalization: Conference Proceedings. Vol. 1 - Chişinău: INCE*, *1*, 298–307.

Eriksen, T. H. (2021). The loss of diversity in the Anthropocene biological and cultural dimensions. *Frontiers in Political Science*, *3*. https://doi.org/10.3389/fpos.2021.743610

European Commission. (2015a). An EU action plan for the circular economy. Com.

European Commision. (2015b). *Communication of 2.12.2015 on an EU action plan for the circular economy*. https://doi.org/10.1017/CBO9781107415324.004

European Commission. (2019). *The European green deal*.

Fargnoli, M., De Minicis, M., & Tronci, M. (2014). Design management for sustainability: An integrated approach for the development of sustainable products. *Journal of Engineering and Technology Management*, *34*, 29–45. https://doi.org/10.1016/j.jengtecman.2013.09.005

Gall, M., Schweighuber, A., Buchberger, W., & Lang, W. R. (2020). Plastic bottle cap recycling—Characterization of recyclate composition and opportunities for design for circularity. *Sustainability*, *12*(24), 10378. https://doi.org/10.3390/su122410378

Garg, A. (2015). Green marketing for sustainable development: An industry perspective. *Sustainable Development*, *23*(5), 301–316. https://doi.org/10.1002/sd.1592

Geissdoerfer, M., Savaget, P., Bocken, N. M. P., & Hultink, E. J. (2017). The circular economy – A new sustainability paradigm? *Journal of Cleaner Production*, *143*, 757–768. https://doi.org/10.1016/j.jclepro.2016.12.048

Ghisellini, P., Cialani, C., & Ulgiati, S. (2016). A review on circular economy: The expected transition to a balanced interplay of environmental and economic systems. *Journal of Cleaner Production*, *114*, 11–32. https://doi.org/10.1016/j.jclepro.2015.09.007

Glavič, P. (2021). Evolution and current challenges of sustainable consumption and production. *Sustainability*, *13*(16), 9379. https://doi.org/10.3390/su13169379

Gordy, L. (2003). *Differential importance of ecolabel criteria to consumers*. Institute for Agriculture and Trade Policy 2105 First Avenue South, Minneapolis, MN 5540, 1–9.

Hofenk, D., van Birgelen, M., Bloemer, J., & Semeijn, J. (2019). How and when retailers' sustainability efforts translate into positive consumer responses: The interplay between personal and social factors. *Journal of Business Ethics*. https://doi.org/10.1007/s10551-017-3616-1

Hysa, E., Kruja, A., Rehman, N. U., & Laurenti, R. (2020). Circular economy innovation and environmental sustainability impact on economic growth: An integrated model for sustainable development. *Sustainability*, *12*(12), 4831. https://doi.org/10.3390/su12124831

Javaid, M., Haleem, A., Singh, R. P., Suman, R., & Gonzalez, E. S. (2022). Understanding the adoption of Industry 4.0 technologies in improving environmental sustainability. *Sustainable Operations and Computers*, *3*, 203–217. https://doi.org/10.1016/j.susoc.2022.01.008

Kabaja, B., Wojnarowska, M., Cesarani, M. C., & Varese, E. (2022). Recognizability of ecolabels on e-commerce Websites: The case for younger consumers in Poland. *Sustainability*, *14*(9), 5351. https://doi.org/10.3390/su14095351

Khan, S. A. R., Yu, Z., & Farooq, K. (2023). Green capabilities, green purchasing, and triple bottom line performance: Leading toward environmental sustainability. *Business Strategy and the Environment*, *32*(4), 2022–2034. https://doi.org/10.1002/bse.3234

Kim, M., & Chung, J. (2018). Sustainable growth and token economy design: The case of Steemit. *Sustainability*, *11*(1), 167. https://doi.org/10.3390/su11010167

Kirchherr, J., Reike, D., & Hekkert, M. (2017). Conceptualizing the circular economy: An analysis of 114 definitions. In *Resources, Conservation and Recycling*. https://doi.org/10.1016/j.resconrec.2017.09.005

Komeijani, M., Ryen, E., & Babbitt, C. (2016). Bridging the gap between eco-design and the human thinking system. *Challenges*, *7*(1), 5. https://doi.org/10.3390/challe7010005

Korhonen, J., Honkasalo, A., & Seppälä, J. (2018). Circular economy: The concept and its limitations. *Ecological Economics*. https://doi.org/10.1016/j.ecolecon.2017.06.041

Le Pochat, S., Bertoluci, G., & Froelich, D. (2007). Integrating ecodesign by conducting changes in SMEs. *Journal of Cleaner Production*, *15*, 671–680.

Lin, C. J., Belis, T. T., & Kuo, T. C. (2019). Ergonomics-based factors or criteria for the evaluation of sustainable product manufacturing. *Sustainability*, *11*(18), 4955. https://doi.org/10.3390/su11184955

Ljungberg, L. Y. (2007). Materials selection and design for development of sustainable products. *Materials and Design*, *28*(2), 466–479. https://doi.org/10.1016/j.matdes.2005.09.006

Luttropp, C., & Lagerstedt, J. (2006). Ecodesign and the ten golden rules: Generic advice for merging environmental aspects into product development. *Journal of Cleaner Production*, *14*(15–16), 1396–1408. https://doi.org/10.1016/j.jclepro.2005.11.022

Maccioni, L., Borgianni, Y., & Pigosso, D. C. A. (2019). Can the choice of eco-design principles affect products' success? *Design Science*, *5*, e25. https://doi.org/10.1017/dsj.2019.24

MacDonald, E. F., & She, J. (2015). Seven cognitive concepts for successful eco-design. *Journal of Cleaner Production*, *92*, 23–36. https://doi.org/10.1016/j.jclepro.2014.12.096

Maris, E., Froelich, D., Aoussat, A., & Naffrechoux, E. (2014). From recycling to eco-design. In *Handbook of recycling* (pp. 421–427). Elsevier. https://doi.org/10.1016/B978-0-12-396459-5.00027-1

Maxwell, D., & van der Vorst, R. (2003). Developing sustainable products and services. *Journal of Cleaner Production*, *11*(8), 883–895. https://doi.org/10.1016/S0959-6526(02)00164-6

McDowall, W., Geng, Y., Huang, B., Barteková, E., Bleischwitz, R., Türkeli, S., … Doménech, T. (2017). Circular economy policies in China and Europe. *Journal of Industrial Ecology*. https://doi.org/10.1111/jiec.12597

Mohammad Ebrahimi, S., & Koh, L. (2021). Manufacturing sustainability: Institutional theory and life cycle thinking. *Journal of Cleaner Production*, *298*, 126787. https://doi.org/10.1016/j.jclepro.2021.126787

Molina-Morales, F. X., & Martínez-Fernández, M. T. (2010). Social networks: Effects of social capital on firm innovation. *Journal of Small Business Management*, *48*(2), 258–279. https://doi.org/10.1111/j.1540-627X.2010.00294.x

Moraga, G., Huysveld, S., Mathieux, F., Blengini, G. A., Alaerts, L., Van Acker, K., … Dewulf, J. (2019). Circular economy indicators: What do they measure? *Resources, Conservation and Recycling*, *146*, 452–461. https://doi.org/10.1016/j.resconrec.2019.03.045

Moreno, M., De los Rios, C., Rowe, Z., & Charnley, F. (2016). A conceptual framework for circular design. *Sustainability (Switzerland)*. https://doi.org/10.3390/su8090937

Murphy, J. (2001). From production to consumption. In *Exploring sustainable consumption* (pp. 39–58). Elsevier. https://doi.org/10.1016/B978-008043920-4/50006-9

Negny, S., Belaud, J. P., Cortes Robles, G., Roldan Reyes, E., & Ferrer, J. B. (2012). Toward an eco-innovative method based on a better use of resources: Application to chemical process preliminary design. *Journal of Cleaner Production*, *32*, 101–113. https://doi.org/10.1016/j.jclepro.2012.03.023

Nowicki, P., Ćwiklicki, M., Kafel, P., Niezgoda, J., & Wojnarowska, M. (2023). The circular economy and its benefits for pro-environmental companies. *Business Strategy and the Environment*. https://doi.org/10.1002/bse.3382

Nowicki, P., Ćwiklicki, M., Kafel, P., & Wojnarowska, M. (2021). Credibility of certified environmental management systems: Results from focus group interviews. *Environmental Impact Assessment Review*, *88*, 106556. https://doi.org/10.1016/j.eiar.2021.106556

Oláh, J., Aburumman, N., Popp, J., Khan, M. A., Haddad, H., & Kitukutha, N. (2020). Impact of Industry 4.0 on environmental sustainability. *Sustainability*, *12*(11), 4674. https://doi.org/10.3390/su12114674

OECD. (2016). *Forum 2016 issues: International collaboration*; https://www.oecd.org/forum/issues/forum-2016-issues-international-collaboration.htm

Ostrom, E. (2007). Sustainable social-ecological systems: An impossibility? *SSRN Electronic Journal*. https://doi.org/10.2139/ssrn.997834

Paparoidamis, N. G., Tran, T. T. H., Leonidou, L. C., & Zeriti, A. (2019). Being innovative while being green: An experimental inquiry into how consumers respond to eco-innovative product designs. *Journal of Product Innovation Management*, *36*(6), 824–847. https://doi.org/10.1111/jpim.12509

Pigosso, D. C. A., Mcaloone, T. C., Pigosso, D. C. A., & Mcaloone, T. C. (2017). Measuring the implementation of ecodesign management practices: A review and consolidation of process-oriented performance indicators. *Journal of Cleaner Production*, *156*, 293–309. https://doi.org/10.1016/j.jclepro.2017.04.049

Pimenov, D. Y., Mia, M., Gupta, M. K., Machado, Á. R., Pintaude, G., Unune, D. R., … Kuntoğlu, M. (2022). Resource saving by optimization and machining environments for sustainable manufacturing: A review and future prospects. *Renewable and Sustainable Energy Reviews*, *166*, 112660. https://doi.org/10.1016/j.rser.2022.112660

Polverini, D. (2021). Regulating the circular economy within the ecodesign directive: Progress so far, methodological challenges and outlook. *Sustainable Production and Consumption*, *27*, 1113–1123. https://doi.org/10.1016/j.spc.2021.02.023

Potting, J., Hekkert, M., Worrell, E., & Hanemaaijer, A. (2017). *Circular economy: Measuring innovation in the product chain.*; https://www.pbl.nl/uploads/default/downloads/pbl-2016-circular-economy-measuring-innovation-in-product-chains-2544.pdf

Prieto-Sandoval, V., Jaca, C., & Ormazabal, M. (2018). Towards a consensus on the circular economy. *Journal of Cleaner Production*, *179*, 605–615. https://doi.org/10.1016/j.jclepro.2017.12.224

Reike, D., Vermeulen, W. J. V., & Witjes, S. (2018). The circular economy: New or Refurbished as ce 3.0? — Exploring controversies in the conceptualization of the circular economy through a focus on history and resource value retention options. *Resources, Conservation and Recycling*, *135*, 246–264. https://doi.org/10.1016/j.resconrec.2017.08.027

Rendtorff, J. D. (2019). Ethics and justice in the international world: The problem of globalization and the need for a cosmopolitan spirit. In *Philosophy of management and sustainability: Rethinking business ethics and social responsibility in sustainable development* (pp. 3–18). Emerald Publishing Limited. https://doi.org/10.1108/978-1-78973-453-920191001

Riskos, K., Dekoulou, P. (Evi), Mylonas, N., & Tsourvakas, G. (2021). Ecolabels and the attitude–behavior relationship towards green product purchase: A multiple mediation model. *Sustainability*, *13*(12), 6867. https://doi.org/10.3390/su13126867

Romer, P. (1994). New goods, old theory, and the welfare costs of trade restrictions. *Journal of Development Economics*, *43*(1), 5–38. https://doi.org/10.1016/0304-3878(94)90021-3

Rosli, T., & Ahmad, F. S. (2019). A review on green trust and environmental quality awareness affect towards environmental attitude. In *Green business* (pp. 1510–1522). IGI Global. https://doi.org/10.4018/978-1-5225-7915-1.ch073

Saidani, M., Yannou, B., Leroy, Y., & Cluzel, F. (2017). How to assess product performance in the circular economy? Proposed requirements for the design of a circularity measurement framework. *Recycling*. https://doi.org/10.3390/recycling2010006

Sanyé-Mengual, E., Lozano, R. G., Farreny, R., Oliver-Solà, J., Gasol, C. M., & Rieradevall, J. (2014). *Introduction to the eco-design methodology and the role of product carbon footprint* (pp. 1–24). https://doi.org/10.1007/978-981-4560-41-2_1

Schumacher, I. (2010). Ecolabeling, consumers' preferences and taxation. *Ecological Economics*, *69*(11), 2202–2212. https://doi.org/10.1016/j.ecolecon.2010.06.005

Sdrolia, E., & Zarotiadis, G. (2019). A comprehensive review for green product term: From definition to evaluation. *Journal of Economic Surveys*. https://doi.org/10.1111/joes.12268

Shuaib, M., Seevers, D., Zhang, X., Badurdeen, F., Rouch, K. E., & Jawahir, I. S. (2014). Product sustainability index (ProdSI). *Journal of Industrial Ecology*, *18*(4), 491–507. https://doi.org/10.1111/jiec.12179

Sołtysik, M., Urbaniec, M., & Wojnarowska, M. (2019). Innovation for sustainable entrepreneurship: Empirical evidence from the Bioeconomy Sector in Poland. *Administrative Sciences*, *9*(3), 50. https://doi.org/10.3390/admsci9030050

Tavares-Lehmann, A. T., & Varum, C. (2021). Industry 4.0 and sustainability: A bibliometric literature review. *Sustainability*, *13*(6), 3493. https://doi.org/10.3390/su13063493

Thøgersen, J., Haugaard, P., & Olesen, A. (2010). Consumer responses to ecolabels. *European Journal of Marketing*, *44*(11), 1787–1810. https://doi.org/10.1108/03090561011079882

UNEP. (2011). Decoupling Natural Resource Use and Environmental Impacts from Economic Growth. In *International Resource Panel.*; https://wedocs.unep.org/handle/20.500.11822/9816

Urbaniec, M., Sołtysik, M., Prusak, A., Kułakowski, K., & Wojnarowska, M. (2021). Fostering sustainable entrepreneurship by business strategies: An explorative approach in the bioeconomy. *Business Strategy and the Environment*. https://doi.org/10.1002/bse.2885

Varese, E., Cesarani, M. C., & Wojnarowska, M. (2023). Consumers' perception of suboptimal food: Strategies to reduce food waste. *British Food Journal*, *125*(1), 361–378. https://doi.org/10.1108/BFJ-07-2021-0809

Wijkman, A., & Skånberg, K. (2015). *The circular economy and benefits for society: Jobs and climate clear winners in an economy based on renewable energy and resource efficiency*. The Club of Rome.

Wojnarowska, M., & Salerno-Kochan, R. (2022). The fourth industrial revolution as an opportunity for the development of a circular economy. In *Industrial revolution 4.0* (pp. 119–142). Routledge. https://doi.org/10.4324/9781003264170-7

Wojnarowska, M., Sołtysik, M., & Ingrao, C. (2022). Characteristics of sustainable products. In *Sustainable products in the circular economy* (pp. 1–17). Routledge. https://doi.org/10.4324/9781003179788-1

Wojnarowska, M., Sołtysik, M., & Prusak, A. (2021). Impact of eco-labelling on the implementation of sustainable production and consumption. *Environmental Impact Assessment Review*, *86*, 106505. https://doi.org/10.1016/j.eiar.2020.106505

WEF. (2016). *Intelligent assets unlocking the circular economy potential*. https://www.weforum.org/publications/intelligent-assets-unlocking-the-circular-economy-potential/

Yi, L., Glatt, M., Sridhar, P., de Payrebrune, K., Linke, B. S., Ravani, B., & Aurich, J. C. (2020). An eco-design for additive manufacturing framework based on energy performance assessment. *Additive Manufacturing*, *33*, 101120. https://doi.org/10.1016/j.addma.2020.101120

Yokokawa, N., Masuda, Y., Amasawa, E., Sugiyama, H., & Hirao, M. (2020). Systematic packaging design tools integrating functional and environmental consequences on product life cycle: Case studies on laundry detergent and milk. *Packaging Technology and Science*, *33*(11), 445–459. https://doi.org/10.1002/pts.2526

Young, W., Hwang, K., McDonald, S., & Oates, C. J. (2010). Sustainable consumption: Green consumer behaviour when purchasing products. *Sustainable Development*, *18*(1), 20–31. https://doi.org/10.1002/sd.394

Yuille, A., Tyfield, D., & Willis, R. (2021). Implementing rapid climate action: Learning from the 'practical wisdom' of local decision-makers. *Sustainability*, *13*(10), 5687. https://doi.org/10.3390/su13105687

Yung, W. K. C., Chan, H. K., Wong, D. W. C., So, J. H. T., Choi, A. C. K., & Yue, T. M. (2012). Eco-redesign of a personal electronic product subject to the energy-using product directive. *International Journal of Production Research*, *50*(5), 1411–1423. https://doi.org/10.1080/00207543.2011.571941

Zeng, T., Durif, F., & Robinot, E. (2021). Can eco-design packaging reduce consumer food waste? an experimental study. *Technological Forecasting and Social Change*, *162*, 120342. https://doi.org/10.1016/j.techfore.2020.120342

4 Sustainable marketing

4.1 Definition of sustainable marketing

Sustainability is gaining increasing attention in the marketing arena. The historical evolution of marketing's sustainability agenda has been described as a journey through a number of different eras: chronologically ordered as ecological marketing in the 1970s; environmental/green marketing in the 1980s and mid-1990s; and sustainability marketing from the mid-1990s onwards (Lloveras et al., 2022; Sharma, 2021; Leonidou & Leonidou, 2011; Chabowski et al., 2011). Sustainable marketing for sustainable development is an increasingly important topic in academic marketing research (Peattie & Collins, 2009, Thøgersen & Schrader, 2012, Zabkar et al., 2018, Harrison et al., 2023), public policy (Eurostat, 2023), and corporate practice (Pucker, 2021). Sustainability has become a priority for more and more brands, and this is reflected in their marketing campaigns. Examples of sustainable brand marketing include Patagonia, with a long history of promoting sustainability, including its "Don't Buy This Jacket" ad on Black Friday in 2011 and its more recent "Buy Less Demand More" campaign, Levi Strauss and Company's "Buy Better, Wear Longer" campaign, which also encourages consumers to reuse and recycle while raising awareness of the environmental impact of apparel production, and LEGO's commitment to make its bricks from more sustainable materials by 2030 and its "Building Instructions for a Better World" campaign (Koeder, 2023).

To understand sustainable marketing, we must first understand sustainable consumption. It is defined as the use of goods and services that satisfy basic needs and provide a better quality of life, minimising the consumption of natural resources, toxic materials, and the emission of wastes and pollutants throughout the life cycle so as not to compromise the needs of future generations (UNEP, 2021). Consumer behaviour is certainly one of the main contributors to current environmental and social problems (Zabkar et al., 2018). Sustainable marketing focuses on consumers, who are expected to behave sustainably and contribute to sustainable development (Hosta & Zabkar, 2021), and on companies, which are expected to recognise and respond to stakeholder expectations by committing to more sustainable activities (Čater et al., 2023).

However, a systematic review of sustainability in the marketing literature shows that there is still a lack of a universally accepted definition of sustainable marketing

DOI: 10.4324/9781032697895-5

(Lunde, 2018). Indeed, the Brundtland Commission's definition of sustainable development (WCED, 1987) and Elkington's (1998) triple bottom line have the major weakness of not being based on the exchange of values, the central concept of the marketing discipline (Alderson, 1957), which has implications for marketing and consumer research. To overcome this weakness, Lunde (2018) defines sustainable marketing as *the strategic creation, communication, delivery, and exchange of offerings that create value through consumer behavior, business practices, and the marketplace while causing less harm to the environment and improving the quality of life and well-being of consumers and global stakeholders in ethical and equitable ways, today and for future generations*. Sustainable marketing includes offerings that are environmentally or socially conscious – better for the planet and society as a whole.

From a brand/company perspective, sustainable marketing offers several advantages. Sustainable brands are *able to attract customers*, especially Millennials and Gen Z consumers who are willing to spend more on sustainable products (Kadic-Maglajlic et al., 2019). In addition, sustainable brands are better able to *attract and retain employees*, as younger workers want to work for companies that share their concern for climate change and social justice (Klimkiewicz & Oltra, 2017). Finally, the benefit of sustainable marketing is *improved brand reputation* (Martín-de Castro, 2021).

However, there are also disadvantages of sustainable marketing in the sense that values such as sustainability and social responsibility can only be communicated effectively if they are actively lived by the company (Szabo & Webster, 2021). Consumers quickly recognise *greenwashing and socialwashing* as empty promises when claims of green marketing or social responsibility do not accurately reflect the company's environmental and socially responsible behaviour. Examples of this can be found in the fashion industry, which causes significant global carbon emissions, global wastewater, and biodiversity loss, as well as labour exploitation and human rights abuses (Crinis, 2019). It is an example of corporate behaviour that prioritizes short-term positive consequences over long-term negative consequences for society and the environment (Rashidi-Sabet & Madhavaram, 2022). An exception could be found in luxury fashion with high-end products that are more durable and have a longer life cycle, an aspect that is often neglected by consumers when buying fashion products (Sun et al., 2021; Busalim et al., 2022). Another drawback of sustainable marketing is found in explicit forms of right-wing anti-consumer thought and action, including resistance to sustainable consumption, prohibitions/bans, and boycotts of media content, companies, and brands. Resistance to sustainable consumption refers to the rejection of environmentally friendly behaviours that serve conservative political, economic, or theological interests (Ferrell, 2021). Prohibitions include enforcing laws and restricting the consumption of entire categories of products and services. In contrast, boycotts organised by large institutions and involving individuals specifically target brands, companies, and/or creative productions. The common denominator of these manifestations of right-wing consumer hostility is engagement with, criticism of, and control over another's consumption behaviour, which negatively impacts marketing systems and alters the marketing mix and the buyer-seller exchange process (Ferrell, 2021).

In terms of theories and methodological norms, economics and psychology have the greatest influence on the fields of marketing and consumer behaviour. From economics and psychology, marketers have adopted the implicit assumption of an individual/consumer as the primary unit of analysis, along with a preference for quantitative, positivist approaches to research (Davies et al., 2020). The contribution of *psychology* to marketing is significant and invaluable, particularly in the area of sustainable consumption and marketing (Donthu et al., 2021). The influence of *economics* on sustainability research remains important, although there is a long-standing debate about the validity of the assumptions of individuals as rational, analytical decision-makers (Bagozzi, 1975). Sheth and Parvatiyar (2020) explain the transition from market-driven to sustainable marketing by pointing to the shift from the invisible hand, consumer focus, to the visible hand, managed markets and sustainability focus. The predominant theories in sustainability research in marketing are the *theory of planned behaviour* (Ajzen, 1991) and ethical decision-making, such as *values*, *beliefs*, and *norms* (Stern et al., 1999), although they have not shown that attitudes can have explanatory power for individuals' behaviour. Some research has shown that behaviour change occurs with the right nudge without changing attitudes or intentions (Davies et al., 2020). Looking also at the social role of sustainable consumer behaviour, the main drivers of sustainable consumer behaviour appear to be subjective norms, social influence, culture, marketing influence, and social media influence (Xiao et al., 2022).

When comparing *traditional and digital contexts*, in the traditional context, scholars prefer to predict sustainable consumer behaviour based on macro-social factors, such as politics and culture, with the theory of planned behaviour being more widely used. In the digital context, trust is crucial and signalling theory and commitment trust theory have received more attention (Xiao et al., 2022).

As many companies are actively engaged in digital transformation, the question of the *relationship between digital transformation and sustainability* is relevant. The digital transformation of modern companies is one of the "seven big problems" of marketing (Jaworski et al., 2016) from the micro perspective of problems in marketing. The macro perspective, on the other hand, would point to "seven wicked problems of marketing systems" (Laczniak & Shultz, 2020), including exploitation of vulnerable consumer segments, technological intrusion into consumer privacy, and barriers to building sustainable consumption. Thus, in the macro view, digital transformation would be considered from the perspective of threats to consumer privacy. On the other hand, sustainable consumption is overlooked among the "seven big problems", although it is considered one of the key problems of the marketing system in the macro view. The relationships between digital transformation and the economic and environmental dimensions of sustainable performance appear to be curvilinear. While digital transformation increases economic performance at an accelerating pace, it shows an inverted U-shaped relationship with environmental performance. Market turbulence also plays an important role. When market turbulence is low, the impact of digital transformation on economic performance accelerates. In contrast, when market turbulence is high, higher digital transformation is associated with poorer environmental performance (Li, 2022).

4.2 Operationalisation of sustainable marketing

Operationalisation of the sustainable marketing construct from the marketing and consumer behaviour literature is based on bibliographic analyses and critical syntheses by Chabowski et al. (2011), Kemper and Ballantine (2019), Leonidou and Leonidou (2011), McDonagh and Prothero (2014), and Press (2021). A notable finding from these reviews is that researchers studying sustainable consumption have placed much more emphasis on environmental than social aspects (Hosta & Zabkar, 2021).

Environmentally/socially responsible sustainable consumer behaviour (Hosta & Zabkar, 2021) is operationalised as follows:

- when there is a choice, I always choose the product that contributes to the least amount of pollution./When I am shopping, I try to buy from companies that are working to improve conditions for their employees.
- whenever possible, I buy products packaged in recyclable containers./I try to buy from companies that hire people with disabilities.
- when I purchase products, I make a conscious effort to buy those products that are low in pollutants./I make an effort to buy products and services from companies that pay all of their employees a living wage.
- when I have a choice between two equal products, I always purchase the one less harmful to the natural environment./When given a chance, I switch to brands where a portion of the price is donated to charity. I do not buy a product if the company that sells it is environmentally irresponsible./I do not buy a product if the company that sells it is socially irresponsible.
- I have switched products for ecological reasons./I have switched products for social reasons.

Leonidou and Leonidou (2011) identify, synthesise, and evaluate existing research focused on environmental marketing and management, with social aspects being only rudimentary in terms of the subject areas covered and the specific issues raised in each area.

- *marketing management aspects* include green attitudes and responses, green product development, green segmentation, green advertising, green logistics, eco-labelling, green brand positioning, and green pricing.
- *environmental management* includes stakeholder management, planning and control, green organisational culture, and environmental change management.
- *environmental corporate strategy* includes production operations, strategic management, and various functions including marketing, finance, and the supply chain.

- *the external regulatory environment* includes environmental regulations, green standards, and the environmental movement.
- *environmental strategy impact* includes the impact of environmental strategies on performance and environmental benchmarking/best practices.
- *corporate response to the environment* includes social responsibility and environmental ethics.
- *environmental advertising* includes environmental claims, consumer attitudes and responses, green washing, environmental friendliness of advertising, and green advertising ethics.

Press (2021) summarises the different approaches to studying sustainability:

1. *the mainstream approach* to marketing research on sustainability (e.g., Clark et al., 2014) focuses on micro aspects of sustainability and neglects the bigger picture. The prevailing view is that business supports the other two elements of sustainability (society and environment). The main goal of business is profit. A typical research question would be how sustainability affects consumer behaviour.
2. *consumer culture theory* (CCT) (e.g., Thompson, 2019) states that sustainability is complex, interconnected, and nuanced. All three dimensions – economic, environmental, and social – are equally important. A typical question would be how consumers experience and engage in sustainable consumption.
3. *macromarketing*. The critical school (e.g., Prothero et al., 2010; Mittelstaedt et al., 2014) asserts that markets are unsustainable because current business models are causing the current problems. Typical research in this area examines macro-level constructs to explain marketing.
4. *strong sustainability research* starts from the premise that the biosphere is the foundation for society and the economy, while value is derived from the coevolutionary interdependencies of stakeholders. Accordingly, a typical question would be how the elements of a sustainable economy work.

The focus of current sustainability research differs from SSR in several dimensions. According to strong sustainability research (Press, 2021), the unit of analysis should not be the individual (consumer, company) but networked actors. Instead of profit as the main goal, exchange systems should create value, with the role of natural capital, for which there is no substitute, being the most important. Understanding of business and consumer behaviour should be based on culturally, socially, and historically embedded practices rather than economic utility and individual choice. Press (2021) recommends interviewing people to collect data. Finally, instead of the capitalist growth model of exchange, an interdependent model should be applied to support the Sustainable Development Goals (SDGs) through production and consumption (Voola et al., 2022).

4.3 Sustainable marketing tools

Sustainable marketing tools refer to tools used in sustainable marketing to influence sustainable consumer and business behaviour in terms of what is good for consumers and the environment/society. Excessive consumption undoubtedly has a negative impact on the natural environment and individual well-being. Therefore, *environmentally responsible behaviour* includes limiting consumption and setting a course for a responsible lifestyle (Kadic-Maglajlic et al., 2019), but also living within one's means and engaging in some form of anti-consumption behaviour (Ziesemer et al., 2021). For example, in reducing car use and intention to reduce car use, *environmental and moral identities are the most important antecedents, along with concern for the environment* (Culiberg et al., 2023). *Environmental concern, past experience, and perceived usefulness* influence green consumer behaviour. On the other hand, *lack of environmental knowledge, high prices, and associated risk* are identified as barriers that create *a gap between consumer attitudes and actual purchase behaviour* towards green products (Sharma, 2021). Moreover, in *socially responsible behaviours*, *social connections* are positively related to young adults' social cause purchase intentions, while *emotion regulation* strengthens this relationship in contexts where young adults have opportunities for socially responsible behaviours (Arslanagic-Kalajdzic et al., 2022). Research also shows that sustainable behaviours are influenced by *social and personal norms, concern about sustainable issues, and consumer awareness* (Hosta & Zabkar, 2021; Koklic et al., 2019). For example, the influential effects of social norms on sustainable behaviours are evident in choices to consume in an environmentally friendly manner, conserve energy, reduce/reuse/recycle, eat sustainable foods, and conserve water (Cialdini & Jacobson, 2021). Managers can therefore promote sustainable behaviours related to environmental and social issues by supporting the development of the factors of norms, concern, and awareness. Emphasising the benefits of sustainable behaviour for increasing consumer happiness (Dhiman & Kumar, 2023) could encourage sustainable consumption, especially among those consumers who do not have positive attitudes towards sustainable consumption (Ramos-Hidalgo et al., 2022).

Companies need to gain insights into the determinants of responsible behaviour because consumers are key stakeholders in the success of companies that implement socially responsible strategies. Two major theoretical frameworks can be presented:

- *the habit-based perspective*, which assumes that behaviours are the result of an automatic response to familiar situations so that habits prevail and rational mechanisms are eliminated.
- *the rationalist perspective*, which assumes that behaviour is the result of a sophisticated cognitive process in which various alternatives are evaluated in light of available information. This perspective can be further subdivided into *attitude–behaviour research* based on expectancy value models, which assumes that consumers make decisions based on expected positive consequences, and research based on *moral norms*, which leads to responsible behaviour.

In addition, *motivation-guided frameworks* are widely used to study the determinants of sustainable behaviour and are a prerequisite for implementing effective marketing strategies based on monetary or non-monetary incentives (Lanzini & Tencati, 2023):

- *the theory of self-determination*, which focuses on motivation as the main driving force shaping behaviour in social contexts, is influenced by individuals striving for autonomy, relatedness, and feelings of competence. Activities are performed because of their *inherent pleasure (intrinsic motivation) or expected separate rewards (extrinsic motivation).*
- *the hierarchy of needs approach* assumes that individual motivation varies according to hierarchically ordered needs, ranging from basic (physiological) to demanding (self-actualisation). The level of needs determines people's ethical behaviour, from concern for immediate needs (e.g., clean water) at the basic level to higher needs once basic needs are satisfied.

  Other theories relate to *social affirmation*, where people make (purchase) decisions based on social pressure from social circles and relatives.
- *role theories* assume that consumers' social position influences their behaviour by creating expectations about what they should (not) do. They focus on consensus (congruence of expectations), conformity (compliance with expected behaviours), role conflict (over incompatible expectations of individual behaviours), and role assumption (connections between a person and his or her participating social interactions).
- *costly signalling theories* suggest that consumers may engage in socially visible behaviours to project the image of individuals who are willing to pay more for the common good (Lanzini & Tencati, 2023).

Since consumers believe that companies should engage in social responsibility, it is important to understand how corporate social responsibility affects consumers' willingness to pay for the goods and services offered by these companies. The results of a systematic literature review (Narayanan & Singh, 2023) confirm the overall positive effect of corporate social responsibility on willingness to pay and the indirect effect between the two, mediated by *brand trust, brand loyalty, brand love, customer satisfaction, brand attitude, purchase intention, and brand equity*. Moderators of the relationship between corporate social responsibility and consumer willingness to pay include *demographic characteristics, cause-related aspects, company characteristics, personal aspects, and product types*. These findings should help marketers develop pricing strategies based on a deeper understanding of consumer behaviour related to perceptions of corporate social responsibility (Narayanan & Singh, 2023).

From a business perspective, sustainability marketing includes sustainable green marketing and design, social sustainability, impact of social and environmental sustainability on economic sustainability, sustainability assessment and business performance, and *strategic corporate social responsibility* (CSR) (Trang et al., 2023). Key corporate social responsibility practices include responsible sourcing and procurement, responsible supplier selection and management, and strategic integration of CSR, and should result in a triple bottom line (social, environmental, and economic) (Huang, et al., 2022). Specific tools for sustainable marketing can be found in *CSR communication* with its stakeholder-focused, business-oriented, and institutionalised framework (Verk, Golob & Podnar, 2021). The main manifestations of sustainable communication include *sustainable/green advertising, sustainability reporting, and (in a negative way) greenwashing* (Golob et al., 2022). Allocating corporate resources to address social, environmental, and governance issues (as part of corporate social responsibility activities) can increase shareholder value and improve financial performance for the benefit of the company and its stakeholders. The impact of corporate social responsibility on corporate financial performance becomes more significant the better the company's environmental, social, and governance (ESG) scores (Coelho et al., 2023).

With the push towards more socially responsive and environmentally sustainable practices, while increasing company value and continuing to be customer-oriented, companies have been forced to implement *sustainable customer relationship management*. This incorporates taking into account social, economic, and environmental impacts, engaging sustainability-conscious customers, and increasing customer awareness while creating long-term customer relations (Ferrer-Estevez et al., 2023). In corporate social responsibility efforts, sustainable marketing strategies should take into account consumer perceptions, as consumers' perception that sustainable strategies are in line with their expectations is an important prerequisite for corporate outcomes (Gleim et al., 2023).

In the area of corporate social responsibility, digital transformation can support companies, especially with regard to environmental protection. The *digitalisation of companies* can have a positive impact by introducing "smart" technologies that allow for the reduction of pollution and the efficient use of natural resources, thus enabling the transformation of business models into more sustainable ones.

4.4 Conclusion

Sustainability is an enduring, complex problem that must be addressed by collective actions and transformations towards sustainability, in which sustainable marketing should play an active role. In line with MacInnis' (2011) framework for conceptual contributions in marketing, Davies et al. (2020) set a research agenda for the field by focusing on alternative consumption models and the development of sustainable people and sustainable markets. According to Press (2021), the research agenda for marketing in sustainability should include functional, integrated definitions, exploring the boundaries of existing research, creating new models and frameworks, building dynamic research streams, and focusing on impact. New models and frameworks should consider interaction holistically and account for extreme resource constraints and sociocultural influences. Finally, impacts should include policy, quality of life, well-being, and socially responsible marketing strategies.

Markets alone cannot address the growing social and environmental challenges. The focus of corporations on their shareholders has led younger generations in particular to worry about environmental degradation, biodiversity loss, income inequality, and climate change (Pucker, 2021). Companies and governments are expected to engage in sustainable marketing. Corporate actions include restructuring the marketing function for sustainability, promoting responsible consumption, rebalancing the marketing mix, and redesigning products and services for sustainable use and reuse. Increased engagement with previously underserved and vulnerable customers can lead to potentially positive outcomes for both businesses and society (Scott & Mende, 2022). On the road to carbon neutrality, many companies are not following through on their promises (Koeder, 2023). Government is expected to provide support programmes, regulatory measures, reform measures, and participatory partnerships with businesses and institutions (Sheth & Parvatiyar, 2020). For example, the European Commission has introduced several initiatives to achieve sustainable development, such as the European Green Deal, the Climate Change Act, and the European Pillar of Social Rights Action Plan (Eurostat, 2023).

The European Commission has an ambitious policy agenda to achieve sustainability in the EU and beyond, with the Sustainable Development Goals (SDGs) and sustainable development at the heart of policymaking (Eurostat, 2023). The United Nations' 17 Sustainable Development Goals (SDGs provide a useful framework for addressing real-world challenges such as poverty, hunger, health, gender equality, education, global warming, the environment, and social justice. The SDGs define global priorities for a sustainable society and are an important focus for sustainable marketing, particularly in the areas of renewable energy, sustainable cities and communities, responsible production and consumption, and climate change mitigation (UN, 2016). UNEP (2021) proposes a holistic approach to sustainable consumption and production based on the following goals: Increasing sustainable management of resources and achieving resource efficiency, including production, distribution, marketing, use, waste management, and reuse of products and services; decoupling environmental degradation from economic growth by reducing resource use, environmental degradation, and pollution, and increasing quality of life; and seizing opportunities for developing countries and "leapfrogging" by creating new markets, green and decent jobs, and resource-efficient, environmentally friendly, and competitive technologies.

It will take problem-oriented research and collaboration among an entire generation of marketing scholars to address the challenges of sustainable marketing. This would likely require more global efforts and interdisciplinary research collaborations to improve our understanding of consumer and manager perceptions and objections to behaviour change (Iacobucci et al., 2020, Harrison et al., 2023). Researchers have both the responsibility to take a stand on sustainability issues and the opportunity to inform policy and develop new marketing strategies for companies facing sustainability issues (Press, 2021). Marketing should be a force for good, meaning sustainable marketing should be used as a catalyst for positive change to promote individual, societal, and environmental well-being (Mende & Scott, 2021). Future research in sustainable marketing should support structural change efforts that ensure stability and prosperity so that we can pass on a better world than the one we inherited.

References

Ajzen, I. (1991). The theory of planned behavior. *Organizational Behavior and Human Decision Processes*, *50*(2), 179–211.

Alderson, W. (1957). *Marketing behavior and executive action: A functionalist approach to marketing theory*. RD Irwin.

Arslanagic-Kalajdzic, M., Kadic-Maglajlic, S., Dlacic, J., & Zabkar, V. (2022). "We go together": Understanding social cause-related purchase intentions of young adults. *Journal of Business Research*, *140*, 130–142. https://doi.org/10.1016/j.jbusres.2021.10.072

Bagozzi, R. P. (1975). Marketing as Exhange. *Journal of Marketing*, *39*(October), 32–39.

Busalim, A., Fox, G., & Lynn, T. (2022). Consumer behavior in sustainable fashion: A systematic literature review and future research agenda. *International Journal of Consumer Studies*, *46*(5), 1804–1828. https://doi.org/10.1111/ijcs.12794

Čater, T., Čater, B., Milić, P., & Žabkar, V. (2023). Drivers of corporate environmental and social responsibility practices: A comparison of two moderated mediation models. *Journal of Business Research*, *159*, 113652. https://doi.org/10.1016/j.jbusres.2023.113652

Chabowski, B., Mena, J., & Gonzalez-Padron, T. (2011). The structure of sustainability research in marketing, 1958–2008: A basis for future research opportunities. *Journal of the Academy of Marketing Science*, *39*(1), 55–70. https://doi.org/10.1007/s11747-010-0212-7

Cialdini, R. B., & Jacobson, R. P. (2021). Influences of social norms on climate change-related behaviors. *Current Opinion in Behavioral Sciences*, *42*, 1–8.

Clark, T., Key, T. M., Hodis, M., & Rajaratnam, D. (2014). The intellectual ecology of mainstream marketing research: An inquiry into the place of marketing in the family of business disciplines. *Journal of the Academy of Marketing Science*, *42*(3), 223–241.

Coelho, R., Jayantilal, S., & Ferreira, J. J. (2023). The impact of social responsibility on corporate financial performance: A systematic literature review. *Corporate Social Responsibility and Environmental Management*, *30*(4), 1535–1560. https://doi.org/10.1002/csr.2446

Crinis, V. (2019). Corporate social responsibility, human rights and clothing workers in Bangladesh and Malaysia. *Asian Studies Review*, *43*(2), 295–312. https://doi.org/10.1080/10357823.2019.1588850

Culiberg, B., Cho, H., Kos Koklic, M., & Zabkar, V. (2023). From car use reduction to ride-sharing: The relevance of moral and environmental identity. *Journal of Consumer Behaviour*, *22*(2), 396–407. https://doi.org/10.1002/cb.2080

Davies, I., Oates, C. J., Tynan, C., Carrigan, M., Casey, K., Heath, T., … Wells, V. (2020). Seeking sustainable futures in marketing and consumer research. *European Journal of Marketing*, *54*(11), 2911–2939. https://doi.org/10.1108/ejm-02-2019-0144

Dhiman, N., & Kumar, A. (2023). What we know and don't know about consumer happiness: Three-decade review, synthesis, and research propositions. *Journal of Interactive Marketing*, *58*(2–3), 115–135. https://doi.org/10.1177/10949968221095548

Donthu, N., Kumar, S., Pattnaik, D., & Lim, W. M. (2021). A bibliometric retrospection of marketing from the lens of psychology: Insights from psychology & marketing. *Psychology and Marketing*, *38*(5), 834–865. https://doi.org/10.1002/mar.21472

Elkington, J. (1997). Cannibals with forks. In *The triple bottom line of 21st century*, 73.

Eurostat. (2023). *Sustainable development in the European Union – Monitoring report on progress towards the SDGs in an EU context* (2023 ed.). Publications Office of the European Union.

Ferrell, L. (2021). Big thinking about marketing. *Journal of Macromarketing*, *41*(4), 527–530. https://doi.org/10.1177/02761467211053533

Ferrer-Estevez, M., & Chalmeta, R. (2023). Sustainable customer relationship management. *Marketing Intelligence and Planning*, *41*(2), 244–262. https://doi.org/10.1108/mip-06-2022-0266

Friedman, M. (1962). *Capitalism and freedom*. University of Chicago Press.
Gleim, M. R., McCullough, H., Sreen, N., & Pant, L. G. (2023). Is doing right all that matters in sustainability marketing? The role of fit in sustainable marketing strategies. *Journal of Retailing and Consumer Services*, *70*. https://doi.org/10.1016/j.jretconser.2022.103124
Golob, U., Podnar, K., & Zabkar, V. (2022). Sustainability communication. *International Journal of Advertising*, 1–10. https://www.tandfonline.com/doi/full/10.1080/02650487.2022.2144035
Harrison, D., Prenkert, F., Hasche, N., & Carlborg, P. (2023). Business networks and sustainability: Past, present and future. *Industrial Marketing Management*, *111*, A10–A17. https://doi.org/10.1016/j.indmarman.2023.03.011
Hosta, M., & Zabkar, V. (2021). Antecedents of environmentally and socially responsible sustainable consumer behavior. *Journal of Business Ethics*, *171*(2), 273–293. https://doi.org/10.1007/s10551-019-04416-0
Huang, Y., Surface, D. L., & Zhang, C. (2022). Corporate social responsibility and sustainability practices in B2B markets: A review and research agenda. *Industrial Marketing Management*, *106*, 219–239. https://doi.org/10.1016/j.indmarman.2022.08.016
Iacobucci, D., Gabriel, M. L., Schneider, M. J., & Hamza, K. M. (2020). Marketing research on environmental sustainability. In *Continuing to broaden the marketing concept: Making the World a Better Place.*Vol. 17 of Review of Marketing Research, 261-292.
Jaworski, B., Malcolm, R., & Morgan, N. (2016, April). 7 Big problems in the marketing industry. *Marketing News*. http://www.ama.org/ publications/MarketingNews/Pages/7-big-problems-marketing. aspx
Kadic-Maglajlic, S., Arslanagic-Kalajdzic, M., Micevski, M., Dlacic, J., & Zabkar, V. (2019). Being engaged is a good thing: Understanding sustainable consumption behavior among young adults. *Journal of Business Research*, *104*, 644–654. https://doi.org/10.1016/j.jbusres.2019.02.040
Kemper, J. A., & Ballantine, P. W. (2019). What do we mean by sustainability marketing? *Journal of Marketing Management*, *35*(3–4), 277–309.
Klimkiewicz, K., & Oltra, V. (2017). Does CSR enhance employer attractiveness? The role of millennial job seekers' attitudes. *Corporate Social Responsibility and Environmental Management*, *24*(5), 449.
Koeder, K. (2023). The future of commerce: Sustainable marketing: Stats, definition, examples. https://www.the-future-of-commerce.com/2022/10/10/sustainable-marketing-definition-examples-benefits/
Koklic, M. K., Golob, U., Podnar, K., & Zabkar, V. (2019). The interplay of past consumption, attitudes and personal norms in organic food buying. *Appetite*, *137*, 27–34. https://doi.org/10.1016/j.appet.2019.02.010
Laczniak, G., & Shultz, C. (2020). Toward a doctrine of socially responsible marketing (SRM): A macro and normative-ethical perspective. *Journal of Macromarketing*, 0276146720963682. https://hbr.org/2023/06/how-brands-can-sell-to-environmentally-conscious-nonconsumers
Lanzini, P., & Tencati, A. (2023). Inside the black box of responsible consumers: Novel perspectives from an integrative literature review. *Business Ethics the Environment & Responsibility*, *32*(2), 847–867. https://doi.org/10.1111/beer.12525
Leonidou, C. N., & Leonidou, L. C. (2011). Research into environmental marketing/management: A bibliographic analysis. *European Journal of Marketing*, *45*(1), 68–103.
Li, L. X. (2022). Digital transformation and sustainable performance: The moderating role of market turbulence. *Industrial Marketing Management*, *104*, 28–37. https://doi.org/10.1016/j.indmarman.2022.04.007

Lloveras, J., Marshall, A. P., Vandeventer, J. S., & Pansera, M. (2022). Sustainability marketing beyond sustainable development: Towards a degrowth agenda. *Journal of Marketing Management, 38*(17–18), 2055–2077. https://doi.org/10.1080/0267257x.2022.2084443

Lunde, M. B. (2018). Sustainability in marketing: A systematic review unifying 20 years of theoretical and substantive contributions (1997–2016). *AMS Review, 8*(3–4), 85–110.

MacInnis, D. J. (2011). A framework for conceptual contributions in marketing. *Journal of Marketing, 75*(4), 136–154.

Martín-de Castro, G. (2021). Exploring the market side of corporate environmentalism: Reputation, legitimacy and stakeholders' engagement. *Industrial Marketing Management, 92*, 289–294. https://doi.org/10.1016/j.indmarman.2020.05.010

McDonagh, P., & Prothero, A. (2014). Sustainability marketing research: Past, present and future. *Journal of Marketing Management, 30*(11–12), 1186–1219.

Mende, M., & Scott, M. L. (2021). May the force be with you: Expanding the scope for marketing research as a force for good in a sustainable world. *Journal of Public Policy and Marketing, 40*(2), 116–125. https://doi.org/10.1177/07439156211000741

Mittelstaedt, J. D., Shultz, C. J., Kilbourne, W. E., & Peterson, M. (2014). Sustainability as megatrend: Two schools of macromarketing thought. *Journal of Macromarketing, 34*(3), 253–264.

Narayanan, S., & Singh, G. A. (2023). Consumers' willingness to pay for corporate social responsibility: Theory and evidence. *International Journal of Consumer Studies*. https://doi.org/10.1111/ijcs.12910

Peattie, K., & Collins, A. (2009). Guest editorial: Perspectives on sustainable consumption. *International Journal of Consumer Studies, 33*(2), 107–112. https://doi.org/10.1111/j.1470-6431.2009.00758.x

Press, M. (2021). Developing a strong sustainability research program in marketing. *AMS Review, 11*(1), 96–114. https://doi.org/10.1007/s13162-020-00185-6

Prothero, A., McDonagh, P., & Dobscha, S. (2010). Is green the new black? Reflections on a green commodity discourse. *Journal of Macromarketing, 30*(2), 147–159.

Pucker, K. P. (2021). Overselling sustainability reporting. *Harvard Business Review, 99*(3), 134–143.

Ramos-Hidalgo, E., Diaz-Carrion, R., & Rodriguez-Rad, C. (2022). Does sustainable consumption make consumers happy? *International Journal of Market Research, 64*(2), 227–248. https://doi.org/10.1177/14707853211030482

Rashidi-Sabet, S., & Madhavaram, S. (2022). A strategic marketing framework for emerging out of the climate change social trap: The case of the fashion industry. *Journal of Macromarketing, 42*(2), 267–291. https://doi.org/10.1177/02761467211058083

Scott, M. L., & Mende, M. (2022). Impact for good: A journey toward impact through marketing scholarship. *European Journal of Marketing, 56*(9), 2573–2585. https://doi.org/10.1108/ejm-03-2022-0153

Sharma, A. P. (2021). Consumers' purchase behaviour and green marketing: A synthesis, review and agenda. *International Journal of Consumer Studies, 45*(6), 1217–1238. https://doi.org/10.1111/ijcs.12722

Sheth, J. N., & Parvatiyar, A. (2020). Sustainable marketing: Market-driving, not market-driven. *Journal of Macromarketing*. https://doi.org/10.1177/0276146720961836

Stern, P. C., Dietz, T., Abel, T., Guagnano, G. A., & Kalof, L. (1999). A value-belief-norm theory of support for social movements: The case of environmentalism. *Human Ecology Review, 6*(2), 81.

Sun, J. J., Bellezza, S., & Paharia, N. (2021). Buy less, buy luxury: Understanding and overcoming product durability neglect for sustainable consumption. *Journal of Marketing, 85*(3), 28–43. https://doi.org/10.1177/0022242921993172

Szabo, S., & Webster, J. (2021). Perceived greenwashing: The effects of green marketing on environmental and product perceptions. *Journal of Business Ethics, 171*(4), 719–739.

Thøgersen, J., & Schrader, U. (2012). From knowledge to action—New paths towards sustainable consumption. *Journal of Consumer Policy*, *35*(1), 1–5.

Thompson, C. J. (2019). The 'big data'myth and the pitfalls of 'thick data'opportunism: On the need for a different ontology of markets and consumption. *Journal of Marketing Management*, *35*(3–4), 207–230.

Trang, P. N. T., Le, A. N. H., Tan, L. P., & Cheng, J. M. S. (2023). Sustainable marketing management: Using bibliographic coupling to review the state-of-The-Art and identify future research prospects. *Journal of Business-to-Business Marketing*, *30*(1), 63–85. https://doi.org/10.1080/1051712x.2023.2188134

UNEP. (2021). Sustainable consumption and production policies. https://www.unep.org/explore-topics/resource-efficiency/what-we-do/sustainable-consumption-and-production-policies

UN. (2016). The 17 goals. https://sdgs.un.org/goals

Verk, N., Golob, U., & Podnar, K. (2021). A dynamic review of the emergence of corporate social responsibility communication. *Journal of Business Ethics*, *168*(3), 491–515.

Voola, R., Bandyopadhyay, C., Voola, A., Ray, S., & Carlson, J. (2022). B2B marketing scholarship and the UN sustainable development goals (SDGs): A systematic literature review. *Industrial Marketing Management*, *101*, 12–32. https://doi.org/10.1016/j.indmarman.2021.11.013

WCED. (1987). *Our common future, the report of the world commission on environment and development*. Oxford University Press.

Xiao, J., Yang, Z., Li, Z., & Chen, Z. (2022). A review of social roles in green consumer behaviour. *International Journal of Consumer Studies*. https://doi.org/10.1111/ijcs.12865

Ziesemer, F., Hüttel, A., & Balderjahn, I. (2021). Young people as drivers or inhibitors of the sustainability movement: The case of anti-consumption. *Journal of Consumer Policy*, 44(3), 427–453.

5 Sustainable entrepreneurship

5.1 Introduction

Business strategies such as "corporate greening" and the "triple bottom line" to promote sustainability have proved insufficiently fast or effective in addressing critical global issues such as climate change (IPCC, 2014), species extinction (Barnosky et al., 2011), and meeting basic human needs (UN, 2013). Climate change has been described as an unprecedented and comprehensive market failure. Despite these challenges, there remains a strong expectation of a "greening" of the economy (OECD, 2011), based largely on the potential for innovation and entrepreneurship (Hall et al., 2010). Entrepreneurship, especially when it leads to disruptive innovation and meaningful change (Schumpeter, 1934), is an important driver of social change. If harnessed to sustainability, it can initiate or reinforce necessary change. In this context, sustainable entrepreneurship (SE) has developed as a field of research that integrates entrepreneurship with sustainable development goals, seeking to meet current needs without compromising the ability of future generations to meet them (Cohen & Winn, 2007; Dean & McMullen, 2007; WCED, 1987).

As Shane and Venkataraman (2000) point out, entrepreneurs are often seen as responding to opportunities. It is therefore crucial to understand the relationship between these opportunities and SE goals. If significant opportunities related to sustainability are not identified or generated, entrepreneurship may not play a significant role in the field. Conversely, the ability to see opportunities to address environmental or poverty issues may be a unique strength of entrepreneurship, especially in the context of widespread social transformation. For example, Cohen and Winn (2007, p. 31) suggest that market failures not only lead to environmental damage but also offer significant prospects for the development of revolutionary technologies and business models. Dean and McMullen (2007, p. 53) also highlight the existence of entrepreneurial opportunities in environmental market imperfections. They link these opportunities to the scale of environmental problems or economic losses resulting from environmental degradation. Based on this viewpoint, the escalating degradation of the Earth's ecosystems may paradoxically translate into increasing opportunities for entrepreneurship.

The concept of sustainable entrepreneurship brings with it some questionable assumptions. The main issue is the narrow view of sustainability challenges (and

DOI: 10.4324/9781032697895-6

corresponding opportunities) solely as market failures. Such a perspective ignores other dimensions of sustainability problems. In addition, these frameworks often implicitly or explicitly rely on concepts of utility and substitutability, which may oversimplify the complex environmental and social dynamics associated with sustainable development. These assumptions may limit the effectiveness and scope of SE in addressing broader sustainability issues.

The market failure perspective advocates the establishment of property rights and appropriate pricing, enabling the creation of efficient markets that recognise the value of services that were previously not priced (Dean & McMullen, 2007). Entrepreneurs are an integral part of this approach, advocating for new norms and practices by presenting sustainable solutions and using innovative methods for further exploitation. Consequently, this viewpoint suggests that entrepreneurs focused on sustainability will operate within the established economic paradigm of private ownership and market transactions. This orientation leads them to deal with issues that lend themselves to market-based solutions, where they can achieve remarkable profits or entrepreneurial rents. Market entrepreneurship has the potential to enhance sustainability by improving productivity, reducing externalities, expanding information, and creating new markets (Cohen & Winn, 2007). However, placing the emphasis solely on markets and their failures risks neglecting issues where the establishment of appropriate market mechanisms is challenging.

Based on these considerations, it becomes evident that although economic information, cost-benefit analysis, and market allocation are important elements in the pursuit of sustainable development, equating the potential of sustainable entrepreneurship (SE) solely with market failures is insufficient. To realise its full potential in the pursuit of sustainable development goals, SE requires a different conceptual framework. This includes a broader understanding of what constitutes opportunities in this context. To reiterate Patzelt and Shepherd (2011), there is potential for theoretical diversity in the emerging field of SE. The aim of this chapter is to analyse the role of entrepreneurship in sustainable development as a new concept for discovering, creating, and exploiting new opportunities to address today's sustainability challenges.

5.2 Conceptualisation of sustainable entrepreneurship

To explain the interplay between entrepreneurship and sustainability, it is necessary to define these concepts, although definitive descriptions remain elusive. Entrepreneurship is commonly understood as the process of starting a business with personal capital, while sustainability is seen as the ability of an organisation to survive by managing its environment. Schaltegger and Wagner (2008) conceptualise sustainable entrepreneurship as the integration of human society and the biosphere or as the intersection of sustainability principles and business practices.

Iyigun (2015) divides sustainability into three interrelated dimensions: (1) social sustainability, which refers to the alignment between a company's values and the needs of its stakeholders; (2) economic sustainability, which refers to an organisation's proficiency in managing capital, funds, and resources; and (3) environmental sustainability, which focuses on the protection of ecosystems. Together, these dimensions shape a broader understanding of sustainability in the context of entrepreneurial ventures.

The common basis of entrepreneurship and sustainability is often framed by the concept of longevity, which includes the creation of sustainable goods, value, or services. This includes the preservation of current resources for future generations (the core principle of sustainability) and the development of long-term, innovative solutions (the hallmark of entrepreneurship). However, in the context of sustainable entrepreneurship, we propose to shift the focus from longevity to impact. Historical trends show that anticipating the needs of future generations is difficult due to their constantly evolving nature. Given the rapid pace of change today, adaptability is crucial. Strictly adhering to the aim of product or service longevity can be unrealistic and, as traditional entrepreneurial theories and practices show, sometimes harmful to the environment. Therefore, sustainable entrepreneurship should emphasise impact rather than longevity, recognising the dynamic and evolving nature of social and environmental needs.

Sustainable entrepreneurship lies "in between for-profit and not-for-profit, in between cash and cause. The main goal of the business activity of the sustainable entrepreneurs should be 'looking for prosperity'" (İyigün, 2015, p. 1230). Sustainable entrepreneurship is characterised by the identification, development, and capitalisation of opportunities that enhance sustainability, bringing social and environmental benefits to society. This definition, provided by Hockerts and Wüstenhagen (2010), Pacheco et al. (2010), and Shepherd and Patzelt (2011), places a strong emphasis on generating positive social impacts.

Central to sustainable entrepreneurship, and entrepreneurship more broadly, is the concept of opportunity creation, as highlighted in the literature (Harms et al., 2009). Cohen and Winn (2007) link the identification of opportunities in sustainable entrepreneurship to market imperfections. These imperfections include inefficiencies of firms, the existence of externalities, flawed pricing mechanisms, and uneven distribution of information. Entrepreneurs who are adept at recognising these market imperfections have greater potential for success, exploiting these gaps for entrepreneurial advantage.

5.3 Opportunities and entrepreneurship

To explore the integration of sustainability with entrepreneurship, it is first necessary to define entrepreneurship as "the scholarly examination of how, by whom, and with what effects opportunities to create future goods and services are discovered, evaluated and exploited" (Shane & Venkataraman, 2000, p. 218). In their influential work, Shane and Venkataraman argued that entrepreneurship occurs at the intersection of opportunities and entrepreneurial individuals. Given the limitations of the market definition of opportunity, this raises an important question: What types of opportunities can drive sustainable entrepreneurship that are compatible with strong sustainability?

5.3.1 Conceptualising entrepreneurial opportunities

The economic underpinnings of entrepreneurship, highlighted by scholars such as Kirzner (1997) and Schumpeter (1934), are evident in Shane and Venkataraman's (2000, p. 220) reference to Casson (1982), where they define entrepreneurial opportunities as "those situations in which new goods, services, raw materials, and organizing methods can be introduced and sold at greater cost than their production". In their comprehensive review of 56 articles to identify a common definition of opportunity, Hansen et al. (2011) deduced that a synthesised definition, encompassing the most common elements, is as follows: "an opportunity is the possibility of introducing a new product to the market at a profit" (Hansen et al., 2011, p. 292). The research area covers a variety of perspectives. In their comprehensive analysis, Hansen et al. (2011) identified as many as 49 different interpretations of the concept of "opportunity". From this broad range, they proposed two distinct composite definitions, seemingly independent of market contexts. The first presents an opportunity as "the ability to develop a solution to a problem", while the second interprets it as "a circumstance in which entrepreneurs can invent or construct a new framework of means and ends". This emphasis on new frameworks of means and ends distinguishes entrepreneurial opportunities from the usual opportunities for economic gain that result from optimising existing means and ends. The latter refers to managerial strategies in which systematic calculations and incremental improvements in production systems prevail over creative innovations. Sustainable entrepreneurship thus goes beyond the scope of mere eco-efficiency implementations in a company, emphasising the importance of innovative approaches in entrepreneurial ventures (Urbaniec, 2018).

5.3.2 Opportunities as market failures

Within sustainable entrepreneurship (SE), there is a consensus, although implicit, similar to traditional theories of entrepreneurship, that entrepreneurs are driven by the potential to earn entrepreneurial rents, as explained by Schaltegger and Wagner (2011). These rents represent returns that are higher than the norm, achievable through the ability of entrepreneurs to recognise opportunities overlooked by other market participants, compounded by the high risk and opportunity costs associated with realising these opportunities, as outlined by Venkataraman (1997). It is widely assumed that entrepreneurs incur lower opportunity costs when taking risks compared with established players, as confirmed by York and Venkataraman (2010).

The SE literature focuses in particular on opportunities arising from environmentally relevant market failures. These failures arise from persistent market imbalances caused by various barriers, as identified by Cohen and Winn (2007) and Dean and McMullen (2007). When individual actors overcome these barriers, not only are there opportunities to profit from entrepreneurship, but markets move towards greater efficiency and sustainability. This process theoretically alleviates environmental issues in a similar way to solving other problems. It is worth noting, however, that while entrepreneurs can exploit these market failures to worsen environmental degradation, the SE literature does not typically address such entrepreneurial actions, as Hall et al. (2010) and York and Venkataraman (2010) have pointed out.

Cohen and Winn (2007) identify four market failures that catalyse opportunities for SE while contributing to environmental issues: suboptimal firm productivity, the prevalence of externalities, flawed pricing mechanisms, and imperfect information distribution. For example, the inefficient use of resources by firms presents an opportunity for technological innovation in which entrepreneurs can play a key role. According to Lovins, Lovins and Hawken (1999), innovation can significantly reduce resource use and waste across industries (Urbaniec et al, 2022). In this scenario, the concept of waste goes beyond mere inefficiency; emissions and waste take on greater importance as externalities, which Cohen and Winn (2007, p. 40) describe as "one of the biggest departures from neoclassical economic assumptions".

Addressing these externalities, for example, by adopting cleaner practices, offers opportunities, especially when new business models and payment systems are developed in collaboration with stakeholders affected by these externalities. Environmental resources, especially those belonging to a common pool, are often undervalued, creating opportunities for SEs to develop alternative uses for resources that also affect market prices and exchange. Furthermore, SE can improve the dissemination of information by establishing environmental standards and labels, thereby educating consumers about the environmental impacts of production, as suggested by Cohen and Winn (2007).

Dean and McMullen (2007) analyse market failures under the classifications of public goods, externalities, monopoly power, inappropriate government intervention, and imperfect information. A characteristic of public goods is their non-excludability, which often leads to their overconsumption. This phenomenon is evident in the overexploitation of various common resources, as illustrated by cases such as excessive carbon emissions or overfishing, as highlighted by Hardin (1968). A market-based approach to this issue involves establishing and enforcing a system of property rights that limits resource use through prices that reflect scarcity. In this area, according to Dean and McMullen (2007), sustainable entrepreneurs have the potential to lead technological advances to establish such systems, effectively transforming a public good into a private one. The solution, however, requires parallel policy efforts to encourage government agencies to adopt and regulate these systems. While privatisation can increase resource efficiency, it does not automatically ensure the sustainability of natural capital protection. This is due to the potential inability of entrepreneurs to accurately define the boundaries of sustainable use.

The literature on sustainable entrepreneurship seems to embrace the concept of entrepreneurs operating outside traditional market boundaries, such as engaging in political advocacy. However, the ultimate goal remains the establishment of a market-based allocation system, which, in turn, facilitates entrepreneurs' annuities as a reward for their efforts. Thus, while SE explicitly recognises the role of the environment and establishes linkages between entrepreneurial opportunities and the biosphere, these linkages are mainly mediated by market mechanisms. In this view, markets are seen both as a source of inefficiency (and thus as a problem) and as a solution when they achieve efficiency.

5.3.3 Exploring or creating opportunities

The discourse on entrepreneurial opportunity has been the subject of considerable academic debate. Sarasvathy (2001) posed a fundamental question: Are opportunities in entrepreneurship actively created by individuals or are they merely discovered? Dutta and Crossan (2005) took a deterministic view, conceptualising entrepreneurial opportunity as a constellation of environmental factors that facilitate the introduction of new products or services into the market. This occurs either through an existing venture or a new venture initiated by an entrepreneur or team of entrepreneurs. This conceptualisation suggests that opportunities can be seen as causal catalysts that initiate entrepreneurial ventures. Developing this discourse further, Chiasson and Saunders (2005) analysed six divergent theoretical perspectives on opportunities. Their analysis showed that structuration theory can provide a comprehensive framework for integrating these different perspectives. According to this theory, entrepreneurial actions generate structures, which, in turn, influence and shape subsequent entrepreneurial actions. This cyclical interaction between actions and structures offers a nuanced understanding of opportunity dynamics in the entrepreneurial process.

The debate about whether opportunities in entrepreneurship are discovered or created has significant practical implications for the field (Urbaniec et al., 2022). Alvarez and Barney (2007) argue that if opportunities are inherently discovered, entrepreneurs should prioritise analysis of markets and industries. This approach usually requires a focus on strategic planning techniques. In this perspective, it is crucial that entrepreneurs possess the competencies required to identify and exploit pre-existing opportunities that come from outside, as Dutta and Crossan (2005) highlight.

Conversely, if the position is that opportunities are created, the entrepreneurial approach changes significantly. In this context, Sarasvathy (2001) suggests that excessive planning at an early stage can be counterproductive. Instead, entrepreneurs should recognise the role of planning primarily as a communication tool. Such an approach is crucial for convincing stakeholders, increasing the legitimacy of the venture, and contributing to the social process of opportunity creation. Thus, understanding the nature of entrepreneurial opportunities – whether discovered or created – requires different strategic approaches and skill sets for effective entrepreneurship.

In sustainable entrepreneurship research, the genesis of opportunities is often attributed to the presence of market failures, which gives these opportunities an objective existence. Hall et al. (2010) go on to explain that such opportunities tend to be outside the scope of dominant market forces. This suggests that conventional market mechanisms may not be adequate to reveal these opportunities. Seeking to identify opportunities within market parameters carries inherent risks, particularly given the challenges posed by traditional markets. To reap the benefits of entrepreneurship in the context of environmental degradation, entrepreneurs often find themselves in a situation where they must either create new markets or improve existing ones. This initiative is essential to successfully navigate and exploit the opportunities available in their fields.

While the dichotomy of creating and discovering entrepreneurial opportunities has mainly been analysed in the context of market failures, this framework can also be insightful in understanding emerging opportunities within the social economy. This perspective becomes more important when considering the tangible aspects of entrepreneurial ventures and their interactions with the biosphere, as exemplified by the recognition and reuse of waste. As Patzelt and Shepherd (2011) point out, entrepreneurs need to develop an understanding of natural systems to effectively identify such opportunities.

5.3.4 Entrepreneurial opportunity processes

In order to fully understand how sustainable entrepreneurs can develop a new framework of activities and aims, it is useful to analyse in detail the activities typically undertaken by entrepreneurs. The literature describes these activities as mainly cognitive, innovative, and related to new ideas or business models. Hansen et al. (2011) define this as a cognitive process involving the recognition of an idea and its transformation into a business concept. In addition, they propose alternative definitions, less related to the market context, such as seeing entrepreneurship as a creative process of generating new alternatives or as a unique form of problem-solving. Although these definitions differ, the cognitive and creative aspects are consistently highlighted as central to entrepreneurial ventures. The potential of entrepreneurship to address the major challenges of sustainable development, as Hall et al. (2010) suggest, depends on harnessing this creative capacity. However, robust sustainable entrepreneurship also includes a level of scepticism about the extent of human ingenuity.

This chapter outlines a conceptualisation of sustainable entrepreneurship. A key challenge in this endeavour stems from the fact that current definitions of entrepreneurship, including social entrepreneurship, tend to assume that sustainability depends on efficient market operations (see Table 5.1).

Sustainable entrepreneurship, which operates independently of market contexts in terms of identifying, creating, or realising opportunities, requires a comprehensive reassessment of core terms and concepts within both traditional and sustainable entrepreneurship paradigms. This reorientation of basic assumptions and aims is in line with the theme of entrepreneurship. It encompasses entrepreneurship as a sophisticated problem-solving approach, particularly effective in dealing with uncertain and complex situations, as explored by Sarasvathy and Venkataraman (2011) and York and Venkataraman (2010). Additionally, this is linked to a renewed perception of innovation as a decisive departure from traditional methods of value creation, as highlighted by Hall et al. (2010) and Schumpeter (1934).

Table 5.1 Opportunities for sustainable entrepreneurship

Theme	*Contemporary view on entrepreneurship and SE*
Understanding entrepreneurial opportunity	Opportunities arise because of market failures and entrepreneurs are motivated in order to obtain entrepreneurial rents. This understanding makes entrepreneurs dependent on markets/market mechanisms.
Discovery or creation	Opportunities are either recognised or created. The SE literature points towards opportunities beyond existing market pull.
Processes related to entrepreneurial opportunity	Cognitive and creative processes are involved in problem-solving

Source: Based on Stål and Bonnedahl (2016).

Sustainability and entrepreneurship are fundamentally linked by the need for innovation. This innovation involves creatively combining existing resources in new ways. Pacheco et al. (2010) define sustainable entrepreneurship as the process of "discovering, creating, evaluating and exploiting opportunities to create future goods and services consistent with the aims of sustainable development" (p. 471).

To conclude, sustainable entrepreneurship is not just about creating economic value; it aims to generate social benefits by identifying and developing opportunities in a landscape marked by uncertainty. This endeavour requires a unique blend of qualities: the ability to take risks, innovative thinking, vigilance, and a strong commitment to ethics. These qualities are essential for entrepreneurs to successfully navigate and make a positive contribution to both the business world and society at large in the context of sustainable development.

5.4 Factors affecting sustainable entrepreneurship

In order to understand the motivations behind individuals' involvement in sustainable entrepreneurial activities, it is important to consider why some entrepreneurs are more inclined towards environmental or social issues, actively incorporating these concerns into their ventures. As with mainstream entrepreneurship, there have been numerous studies in the literature aiming to identify the driving forces behind sustainable entrepreneurship, both at individual and organisational levels.

Drawing on the existing literature, these driving forces can be categorised based on their origin:

- internal factors include personal motivations such as deeply held beliefs or concerns about social and environmental issues and the desire to be self-employed.
- external factors include elements such as market failures that may prompt the identification of new opportunities, as well as networks, social capital, and social acceptance.

This division helps to provide a comprehensive understanding of the multi-faceted nature of the motivations that drive sustainable entrepreneurial ventures.

Ajzen (1991) argues that individuals who show an intention towards a particular behaviour tend to show a positive evaluation or what is commonly referred to as a "positive attitude" towards that behaviour. This means that an individual's attitude significantly influences their intention to act in a certain way. Numerous studies in the existing literature have identified attitude as a key determinant of entrepreneurial intention. For example, the study by do Paço, Ferreira, Raposo, Rodrigues, and Dinis (2011) supports this view.

In the context of environmental practices, the role of attitude becomes even clearer. Tonglet, Philips, and Read (2004) identified attitudes towards sustainability as a major predictor of pro-environmental intentions. Similarly, Schick, Marxen, and Freimann (2005) identified it as a key factor influencing the implementation of sustainability practices in the business environment. Consequently, it can be inferred that sustainability-oriented attitudes are a predictor of sustainable entrepreneurial intentions. An individual's behaviour is particularly influenced by social pressure, as explained by Ajzen (1991), who emphasised that social pressure or "social norms" play a key role in determining an individual's decision to engage in a particular behaviour. Essentially, the influence exerted by others in society can significantly shape a person's intention to adopt certain behaviours. This relationship has been confirmed in the context of entrepreneurial intentions. Research by Moriano, Gorgievski, Laguna, Stephen, found that social norms are significantly and positively correlated with entrepreneurial intentions. Regarding sustainable behaviour, the literature shows that social pressure, including the opinions of other individuals or groups, has a significant impact on sustainability intentions.

Furthermore, the relationship between social norms and ecological behavioural intentions has been confirmed to be significant and positive. Meek, Pacheco, and York (2010) also confirmed the importance of social norms in influencing entrepreneurial environmental actions. It can therefore be concluded that social norms are a significant predictor of an individual's propensity towards sustainable entrepreneurship. Perceptions are crucial in shaping individuals' behavioural intentions, particularly in relation to entrepreneurship. Research by Liñán, Rodríguez-Cohard, and Rueda-Cantuche (2005) highlights "perceived desirability" and "perceived feasibility" as key factors influencing entrepreneurial behaviour. Perceived attractiveness refers to the attractiveness of the behaviour, while perceived feasibility refers to the individual's belief in his or her abilities. Research has shown that perceived attractiveness significantly influences venture creation and self-employment decisions (Segal et al., 2005), as well as entrepreneurial intentions (Fitzsimmons & Douglas, 2011).

Gyaneshwar and Nagendra (2017) examined the motivators behind sustainable entrepreneurship, identifying factors such as environmental awareness, market opportunities, entrepreneurial autonomy, livelihood, and personal passion. These elements are considered internal environmental factors. In addition, external environmental influences such as green marketing strategies, government involvement, and green thinking are highlighted.

Regarding external factors, several researchers have highlighted the key role of social acceptance in the entrepreneurial process, a concept distinct from peer pressure, which also has a significant impact. O'Neil and Ucbarasan (2016) explored the concept of legitimacy through a qualitative study involving six emerging businesses. They identified legitimacy as a key factor in engaging stakeholders and increasing the potential for success. However, they also noted that achieving legitimacy can sometimes require entrepreneurs to compromise their initial motivations.

In the context of small and medium-sized enterprises (SMEs), Uhlaner et al. (2010), in their study of 2,000 Dutch companies, found that family businesses tend to adopt more sustainable practices. This tendency is attributed to the entrepreneurs' close ties to local communities and concern for the family's reputation. Similarly, Bianchi and Noci (1998), in their qualitative study of 46 firms, recognised the importance of legitimacy for environmentally friendly firms and maintaining a "green image". They noted that for SMEs, the pressure to achieve legitimacy is generally less intense compared with larger firms. Nicholls (2010) also highlights the importance of legitimacy in the field of social entrepreneurship, further confirming its relevance across different fields of entrepreneurship. In a qualitative study of 44 companies from four different countries, also linked institutional context to "sustainable will". The importance of institutions has been confirmed by several researchers and is discussed later in this review. Another feature worth special attention is the financial factor.

Koe et al. (2014) examined the relationship between sustainable small and medium-sized enterprises (SMEs) and their propensity for sustainable entrepreneurship. They identified four key factors that positively correlate with this propensity: (1) sustainable attitudes, reflecting an individual's environmental awareness; (2) social norms, indicating social pressure to engage in environmentally responsible behaviour; (3) perceived desirability, which refers to an individual's perceived attractiveness of a particular behaviour; and (4) perceived feasibility, which refers to an individual's assessment of his or her own capabilities, closely related to self-efficacy and the propensity to be self-employed.

As previous research confirms, attitude is not only important in determining entrepreneurial intentions (do Paço et al., 2011) but also sustainability behaviour (Schick et al., 2005). Therefore, fostering a positive attitude towards sustainability among SME operators is definitely needed in the development of sustainable entrepreneurship. Koe et al. (2014) further explain that social norms have a significant impact on both entrepreneurial and sustainable behaviour. Their results highlight that all four factors together contribute to the propensity for sustainable entrepreneurship among SMEs.

Furthermore, Gholamhossein and Ali (2016) in their study identified several key factors influencing sustainable entrepreneurship in SMEs, including customer orientation, staff training, human resources, and social support. Pacheco et al. (2010) noted that technological advances and general innovation have changed the approach to entrepreneurship. To create an environmentally friendly business, they suggest that entrepreneurs should initially focus on shaping consumer attitudes towards green products, fostering a belief in the company's commitment to environmental sustainability. Such an approach is crucial to embedding a green culture in a business framework.

5.5 Benefits and challenges related to sustainable entrepreneurship

Integrating sustainability into business operations offers many benefits for entrepreneurs and their companies. Key benefits include (Terán-Yépez et al., 2020; Dodo et al., 2017; Schaltegger et al., 2018):

- increased efficiency and cost reduction: Adopting sustainable practices, such as minimising waste, conserving energy, using resources more efficiently, and choosing environmentally friendly materials, often leads to lower operating costs and increased overall productivity.
- improved brand reputation: Commitment to sustainable practices can significantly improve a company's reputation, fostering consumer loyalty. At a time when consumers are increasingly looking for brands that reflect their personal values, a commitment to sustainability can set a company apart from the competition.
- attracting and retaining talent: Sustainability is an increasingly important priority among employees. Companies that adopt sustainable practices are more likely to attract and retain top talent, especially those employees who want to contribute to positive environmental and social change.
- strengthened stakeholder relationships: As awareness of the environmental and social impacts of business operations increases, integrating sustainability can strengthen relationships with key stakeholders, including customers, suppliers, and the community. This approach demonstrates a genuine commitment to their welfare.
- long-term business viability: Considering the long-term environmental and social consequences of business operations is critical to ensuring ongoing profitability and success.

Therefore, integrating sustainability into business practices is not just a moral or environmental issue, it offers significant business benefits and ensures companies' continued success.

Integrating sustainable practices into entrepreneurship, while beneficial, comes with several significant challenges (Bell & Stellingwerf, 2012; Olateju et al., 2020):

- up-front investment: Switching to sustainable practices, such as using green materials, minimising waste, and optimising energy consumption, often involves significant up-front costs. This financial requirement can be a significant barrier, especially for smaller or newer ventures.
- resistance to organisational change: Changing established business processes and practices with the aim of aligning them with sustainability principles can encounter resistance. This resistance may come from employees, management, or other stakeholders accustomed to traditional methods.

- gap in knowledge and experience: Many entrepreneurs may lack the necessary knowledge or experience to effectively implement sustainable practices. This gap can hinder the initiation or effective implementation of sustainability strategies.
- resource constraints: Entrepreneurs, especially those with limited resources, may find it difficult to invest in the necessary tools and technologies for sustainability, such as energy-efficient systems or renewable energy sources.
- competitive pressures: In some industries, adopting sustainable practices can temporarily put a company at a competitive disadvantage compared with peers who do not make the same sustainability commitments.

Despite these obstacles, many businesses have successfully navigated these challenges and integrated sustainability into their operations, reaping long-term benefits. By recognising and strategically dealing with these challenges, entrepreneurs can prepare their businesses for sustainable success and resilience.

Sustainability is increasingly influencing consumer behaviour and purchasing choices (Mancini et al., 2017). With increasing public awareness of environmental and social issues, more and more consumers are seeking products and services that resonate with their personal values and beliefs. A significant segment of consumers is willing to pay a higher price for products and services that are environmentally and socially responsible. This shift is generating increased demand for sustainable options, benefiting companies committed to these practices. Demonstrating a strong commitment to sustainability can significantly improve a brand's reputation and increase customer loyalty. Consumers prefer brands that reflect their values and are perceived as responsible and ethical. However, companies that neglect sustainability may face negative reactions from consumers, leading to a potential drop in sales and loss of reputation. In conclusion, the role of sustainability in shaping consumer behaviour and purchasing decisions is huge. With an increasing number of consumers paying attention to the environmental and social impact of their purchases, it is crucial for companies to recognise the importance of sustainability and its impact on their success and longevity.

Several companies have achieved significant success by integrating sustainability into their business models, demonstrating that environmental awareness and profitability can go hand in hand. Well-known in the outdoor clothing industry, Patagonia places a high value on sustainability as a key element of its brand identity. The company's practices include using recycled materials, minimising its environmental footprint, and actively supporting environmental aims. This commitment has earned Patagonia a loyal customer base and a reputation as a leader in corporate responsibility (Rattalino, 2018). A pioneer in the automotive sector, Tesla's electric vehicles epitomise the combination of sustainability and cutting-edge technology. Beyond cars, Tesla's investments in renewable energy and energy storage solutions put it at the forefront of the sustainable energy revolution. These companies exemplify how incorporating sustainability into core business practices can bring not only environmental and social benefits but also great business success. They serve as role models for entrepreneurs aspiring to follow a sustainable business path.

5.6 Conclusions

In practice, the importance of sustainable entrepreneurship (SE) is growing among various actors, including international organisations, corporations, and academic institutions. A key moment was the endorsement of the "Development Agenda 2030" by the United Nations (UN) in 2015. This agenda fostered global cooperation across sectors and levels of governance, resulting in increased institutional support for SE initiatives by companies (Schaltegger et al., 2018). In particular, sectors such as agribusiness, construction, and energy are at the forefront, with an increasing focus on assessing the environmental and health impacts of their production policies, as well as financial.

At the same time, the academic world is responding to this trend. Universities now offer specialised programmes in SE, with examples including MBA programmes at the University of Vermont and master's programmes at the University of Bath. In addition, dedicated academic centres focusing on SE have emerged, such as the Centre for Sustainable Entrepreneurship at the University of Groningen, reflecting the growing academic interest and investment in the field.

Moving beyond the traditional boundaries between civil society, politics, and markets, sustainable entrepreneurship offers a multidimensional approach to socio-economic action (York & Venkataraman, 2010). Such entrepreneurial initiatives can manifest themselves in a variety of forms: some may influence policy-making, others may engage in markets, exerting regulatory control or shaping consumer behaviour.

Furthermore, these ventures may create community-based institutional frameworks. This framework uses a combination of formal and informal rules, norms, and social structures with the aim of effectively managing the use of natural capital. This approach challenges the conventional market-centric view of the role of people solely as consumers. Instead, it advocates a broader perspective of well-being, in which sustainability is assessed through various dimensions of value, not just monetary indicators. This paradigm shift also requires moving beyond an individualistic focus on entrepreneurs and market actors. It proposes adopting democratic decision-making processes that are transparent and inclusive, encompassing a wide range of actors and perspectives.

In the sustainability literature, the widespread use of the "triple-bottom-line" metaphor serves to contextualise the lofty ideals of sustainability in the corporate sphere. However, given the lofty expectations of entrepreneurship as a catalyst for profound and necessary change, a more robust set of principles is warranted. Therefore, there is an ongoing need for conceptual development in the context of various sustainable entrepreneurial ventures to better understand their practical implications.

Governments and policy frameworks play a key role in supporting sustainability in the entrepreneurial environment. Governments can motivate companies to adopt sustainable practices by offering tax breaks, financial subsidies, and other incentives. This approach can make sustainability initiatives more viable for businesses. By setting and enforcing environmental standards and regulations, governments force companies to operate in a sustainable manner. This may include mandates to reduce carbon emissions, use environmentally friendly materials, or follow waste management protocols. Government-led campaigns and education programmes can also increase public understanding and appreciation of sustainability. This increased awareness can then increase consumer demand for sustainable products and services, stimulating entrepreneurship in this area. Furthermore, governments can offer necessary resources, such as grants and low-interest loans, to support entrepreneurs in implementing sustainable strategies in their ventures. To conclude, governments play a key role in shaping an ecosystem conducive to sustainable entrepreneurship. Through various policies and support mechanisms, they can significantly influence the development and success of sustainable business practices.

The trajectory of sustainability in entrepreneurship is extremely promising and has far-reaching implications for society. The growing adoption of sustainable practices by businesses is likely to lead the economy as a whole to greater sustainability and resilience. This shift is expected to create a more environmentally conscious and equitable future. The growing demand for sustainable products and services is also expected to spur creativity and innovation in the business community. This trend is expected to catalyse innovative solutions to environmental challenges, thereby driving progress and development. Sustainable business, by prioritising waste reduction, pollution control, environmental efforts, and energy efficiency, can significantly improve global living standards. By supporting local economies and community-focused initiatives, sustainable entrepreneurial practices can strengthen community resilience and cohesion. As sustainable practices gain popularity in the business world, there is likely to be a paradigm shift towards a more responsible and sustainable corporate culture. This evolution will contribute to a more sustainable future for both humanity and the planet. The role of sustainability in entrepreneurship is not only crucial, it also transformational, with significant potential for positive social impact. Entrepreneurs who integrate sustainability into their business ethos are at the forefront of shaping a more sustainable and prosperous future.

In conclusion, sustainability requires companies to integrate sustainable practices into their business models. This integration not only positively impacts the environment and communities but also contributes to overall social well-being. Integrating sustainable practices offers numerous benefits, including stimulating innovation, improving quality of life, strengthening social ties, and promoting a more responsible business culture. However, there are challenges to implementing sustainable practices. Companies are advised to adopt a number of best practices to effectively address these challenges. These include starting with feasible steps, conducting comprehensive sustainability assessments, actively engaging employees in sustainable initiatives, fostering collaboration with other companies, transparently communicating their commitment to sustainability, and continuously monitoring and improving their sustainability strategy. Looking to the future, the outlook for business sustainability is particularly optimistic and has significant potential to positively shape the future. Therefore, the integration of sustainable practices into business ventures is not only necessary but actually essential to creating a more sustainable and improved world.

References

Alvarez, S., & Barney, J. (2007, November). Discovery and creation: Alternative theories of entrepreneurial action. *Strategic Entrepreneurship Journal*, *26*, 11–26. https://doi.org/10.1002/sej

Barnosky, A. D., Matzke, N., Tomiya, S., Wogan, G. O. U., Swartz, B., Quental, T. B., … Ferrer, E. A. (2011). Has the Earth's sixth mass extinction already arrived? *Nature*, *471*(7336), 51–57. https://doi.org/10.1038/nature09678

Bell, J., & Stellingwerf, J. (2012). *Sustainable entrepreneurship: The motivations and challenges of sustainable entrepreneurs in the renewable energy industry*. https://www.diva-portal.org/smash/record.jsf?pid=diva2%3A536383&dswid=3270

Bianchi, R., & Noci, G. (1998). "Greening" SMEs' competitiveness. *Small Business Economics*, *11*(3), 269–281.

Bocken, N. M. P., Short, S. W., Rana, P., & Evans, S. (2014). A literature and practice review to develop sustainable business model archetypes. *Journal of Cleaner Production*, *65*, 42–56. https://doi.org/10.1016/j.jclepro.2013.11.039

Casson, M. (1982). The theory of foreign direct investment. In *International capital movements: Papers of the fifth annual conference of the international economics study group* (pp. 22–57). Palgrave Macmillan.

Chiasson, M., & Saunders, C. (2005). Reconciling diverse approaches to opportunity research using the structuration theory. *Journal of Business Venturing*, *20*(6), 747–767.

Cohen, B., & Winn, M. I. (2007). Market imperfections, opportunity and sustainable entrepreneurship. *Journal of Business Venturing*, *22*(1), 29–49. http://doi.org/10.1016/j.jbusvent.2004.12.001

Dean, T. J., & McMullen, J. S. (2007). Toward a theory of sustainable entrepreneurship: Reducing environmental degradation through entrepreneurial action. *Journal of Business Venturing*, *22*(1), 50–76. http://doi.org/10.1016/j.jbusvent.2005.09.003

Dodo, F., Potluri, R. M., & Gazara, S. (2017). Sustainable entrepreneurship among rural women in Nigeria: An assessment of benefits. *The Journal of Industrial Distribution & Business*, *8*(3), 5–9.

do Paço, A. M. F., Ferreira, J. M., Raposo, M., Rodrigues, R. G., & Dinis, A. (2011). Behaviors and entrepreneurial intention: Empirical findings about secondary students. *Journal of International Entrepreneurship*, *9*(1), 20–38.

Dutta, D., & Crossan, M. (2005). The nature of entrepreneurial opportunities: Understanding the proces using the 4I organizational learning framework. *Entrepreneurship: Theory and Practice*, *29*(4), 425–449.

Fitzsimmons, J. R., & Douglas, E. J. (2011). Interaction between feasibility and desirability in the formation of entrepreneurial intentions. *Journal of Business Venturing*, *26*(4), 431–440.

Georgescu-Roegen, N. (1993, originally 1971). The entropy law and the economic problem. In H. E. Daly & K. https://www.taylorfrancis.com/chapters/edit/10.4324/9780203830413-2/entropy-law-economic-problem-1970-nicholas-georgescu-roegen

Gholamhossein, H., & Ali, R. (2016). Factors influencing sustainable entrepreneurship in small and medium-sized enterprises in Iran: A case study of food industry. *Sustainability*, *8*, Article Number: 1010.

Gyaneshwar, S. K., & Nagendra, K. S. (2017). Factors influencing young entrepreneurial aspirant's insight towards sustainable entrepreneurship. *Iranian Journal of Management Studies (IJMS)*, *10*(2), 435–466.

Hall, J. K., Daneke, G. A., & Lenox, M. J. (2010). Sustainable development and entrepreneurship: Past contributions and future directions. *Journal of Business Venturing*, *25*(5), 439–448. http://doi.org/10.1016/j.jbusvent.2010.01.002

Hansen, D. J., Shrader, R., & Monllor, J. (2011). Defragmenting definitions of entrepreneurial opportunity. *Journal of Small Business Management*, *49*(2), 283–304.

Hardin, G. (1968). The tragedy of the commons. *Science*, *162*(3859), 1243–1248.

Harms, R., Schulz, A., Kraus, S., & Fink, M. (2009). The conceptualisation of 'opportunity' in strategic management research. *International Journal of Entrepreneurial Venturing, 1*(1), 57–71.

Hockerts, K., & Wüstenhagen, R. (2010). Greening Goliaths versus emerging Davids—Theorizing about the role of incumbents and new entrants in sustainable entrepreneurship. *Journal of Business Venturing, 25*(5), 481–492.

IPCC. (2014, November 1). Climate change 2014. Synthesis report. Approved summary for policymakers (subject to copy editing and lay out). Retrieved November 22, 2014, from www.ippc.ch

İyigün, N. Ö. (2015). What could entrepreneurship do for sustainable development? A corporate social responsibility-based approach. *Procedia-Social and Behavioral Sciences, 195*, 1226–1231.

Kallio, T., & Nordberg, P. (2007, July). "Rationalizing sustainable development" – A critical treatise. *Sustainable Development, 51*, 41–51. https://doi.org/10.1002/sd

Kirzner, I. M. (1997). Entrepreneurial discovery and the competitive market process: An Austrian approach. *Journal of Economic Literature, 35*(1), 60–85.

Koe, W. L., Omar, R., & Majid, I. A. (2014). Factors associated with propensity for sustainable entrepreneurship. *Procedia-Social and Behavioral Sciences, 130*, 65–74.

Liñán, F., Rodríguez-Cohard, J. C., & Rueda-Cantuche, J. M. (2005). Factors affecting entrepreneurial intention levels. *45th Congress of the European Regional Science Association, 23–27 August 2005* (pp. 14769–14774).

Lovins, A., Lovins, L., & Hawken, P. (1999). A road map for natural capitalism. *Harvard Business Review, 77*(3), 145–158.

Mancini, P., Marchini, A., & Simeone, M. (2017). Which are the sustainable attributes affecting the real consumption behaviour? Consumer understanding and choices. *British Food Journal, 119*(8), 1839–1853.

Maradin, D., Malnar, A., & Kaštelan, A. (2022). Sustainable and clean energy: The case of tesla company1. *Journal of Economics, Finance and Management Studies, 5*(12), 3531–3542.

Meek, W. R., Pacheco, D. F., & York, J. G. (2010). The impact of social norms on entrepreneurial action: Evidence from the environmental entrepreneurship context. *Journal of Business Venturing, 25*(5), 493–509.

OECD. (2011). *Towards green growth*. OECD Publishing.

Olateju, A. O., Danmola, R. A., & Aminu, A. W. (2020). Sustainable entrepreneurship and sustainable development in Nigeria: Prospects and challenges. *International Journal of Research and Innovation in Social Science, 4*(11), 372.

O'Neil, I., & Ucbasaran, D. (2016). Balancing "what matters to me" with "what matters to them": Exploring the legitimation process of environmental entrepreneurs. *Journal of Business Venturing, 31*(2), 133–152.

Pacheco, D. F., Dean, T. J., & Payne, D. S. (2010). Escaping the green prison: Entrepreneurship and the creation of opportunities for sustainable development. *Journal of Business Venturing, 25*(5), 464–480.

Patzelt, H., & Shepherd, D. A. (2011). Recognizing opportunities for sustainable development. *Entrepreneurship: Theory and Practice, 35*(4), 631–652. https://doi.org/10.1111/j.1540-6520.2010.00386.x

Rattalino, F. (2018). Circular advantage anyone? Sustainability-driven innovation and circularity at Patagonia, Inc. *Thunderbird International Business Review, 60*(5), 747–755.

Sarasvathy, S. (2001). Causation and effectuation: Toward a theoretical shift from economic inevitability to entrepreneurial contingency. *Academy of Management Review*. http://amr.aom.org/content/26/2/243.short

Sarasvathy, S., & Venkataraman, S. (2011). Entrepreneurship as method: Open questions for an entrepreneurial future. *Entrepreneurship: Theory and Practice, 35*(1), 113–135. https://doi.org/10.1111/j.1540-6520.2010.00425.x

Schaltegger, S., Beckmann, M., & Hockerts, K. (2018). Sustainable entrepreneurship: Creating environmental solutions in light of planetary boundaries. *International Journal of Entrepreneurial Venturing*, *10*(1), 1–16.

Schaltegger, S., & Wagner, M. (2011). Sustainable entrepreneurship and sustainability innovation: Categories and interactions. *Business Strategy and the Environment*, *237*(20), 222–237. http://onlinelibrary.wiley.com/doi/10.1002/bse.682/full

Schaltegger, S., & Wagner, T. (2008). Types of sustainable entrepreneurship and conditions for sustainability innovation: From the administration of a technical challenge to the management of an entrepreneurial opportunity. In R. Wüstenhagen, J. Hamschmidt, S. Sharma, & M. Starik (Eds.), *Sustainable innovation and entrepreneurship* (pp. 27–48). https://www.elgaronline.com/edcollchap/9781847200372.00009.xml

Schick, H., Marxen, S., & Freimann, J. (2005). Sustainability in the start-up process. In M. Schaper (Ed.), *Making ecopreneurs: Developing sustainable entrepreneurship* (pp. 108–121). Ashgate Publishing.

Schumpeter, J. A. (1934). *The theory of economic development*. Harvard University Press.

Segal, G., Borgia, D., & Schoenfeld, J. (2005). The motivation to become an entrepreneur. *International Journal of Entrepreneurial Behavior and Research*, *11*(1), 42–57.

Shane, S., & Venkataraman, S. (2000). The promise of entrepreneurship as a field of research. *Academy of Management Review*, *25*(1), 217–226. Retrieved from http://www.jstor.org/stable/10.2307/259271

Shepherd, D. A., & Patzelt, H. (2011). The new field of sustainable entrepreneurship: Studying entrepreneurial action linking "what is to be sustained" with "what is to be developed." *Entrepreneurship: Theory and Practice*, *35*(1), 137–163. https://doi.org/10.1111/j.1540-6520.2010.00426.x

Stål, H. I., & Bonnedahl, K. (2016). Conceptualizing strong sustainable entrepreneurship. *Small Enterprise Research*, *9*. https://doi.org/10.1080/13215906.2016.1188718

Terán-Yépez, E., Marín-Carrillo, G. M., del Pilar Casado-Belmonte, M., & de las Mercedes Capobianco-Uriarte, M. (2020). Sustainable entrepreneurship: Review of its evolution and new trends. *Journal of Cleaner Production*, *252*, 119742.

Tonglet, M., Phillips, P. S., & Read, A. D. (2004). Using the theory of planned behaviour to investigate the determinants of recycling behaviour: A case study from Brixworth, UK. *Resources, Conservation and Recycling*, *41*(3), 191–214.

Uhlaner, L. M., Berent, M. M., Jeurissen, R. J., & de Wit, G. (2010). Family ownership, innovation and other context variables as determinants of sustainable entrepreneurship in SMEs: An empirical research study. *EIM Research Reports, Reference H, 201006*, pp. 1–29.

UN. (2013). *The millennium development goals report 2013*. United Nations.

Urbaniec, M. (2018). Sustainable entrepreneurship: Innovation-related activities in European enterprises. *Polish Journal of Environmental Studies*, *27*(4), 1773–1779.

Urbaniec, M., Sołtysik, M., Prusak, A., Kułakowski, K., & Wojnarowska, M. (2022). Fostering sustainable entrepreneurship by business strategies: An explorative approach in the bioeconomy. *Business Strategy and the Environment*, *31*(1), 251–267.

Venkataraman, S. (1997). The distinctive domain of entrepreneurship research. *Advances in Entrepreneurship, Firm Emergence and Growth*, *3*(1), 119–138.

World Commission on Environment and Development (WCED). (1987). *Our common future*. Oxford University Press.

York, J. G., & Venkataraman, S. (2010). The entrepreneur–environment nexus: Uncertainty, innovation, and allocation. *Journal of Business Venturing*, *25*(5), 449–463. http://doi.org/10.1016/j.jbusvent.2009.07.007

6 Sustainable innovation

6.1 Introduction

The term "sustainable" gained importance after the publication of "Our Common Future", a landmark report issued in 1987 by the World Commission on Environment and Development (WCED). The WCED set out a definition of sustainable development, stating that it represents a form of development that "meets the needs of the present without compromising the ability of future generations to meet their own needs". Since then, this definition has become a staple of the sustainable development discourse. Sustainable development aims to improve the quality of life around the world while respecting and acting within the limits of the ecosystem (Baumgartner, 2011). This definition captures the essence of the concept but leaves unanswered the key question of its implementation. Koho et al. (2011) stated that its main purpose is to meet human needs, arguing that economic growth is necessary in regions that lack basic resources. They also stressed that such development should not threaten vital natural systems – the atmosphere, water, soil, and living organisms. Reinforcing these views, Murphy (2012) reiterated the age-old paradigm of the triple bottom line, defining sustainable development as the pursuit of a balance between the pillars of environmental, economic, and social sustainability.

Building on more than two decades of various activities, the United Nations has announced 17 Sustainable Development Goals (SDGs) comprising 169 specific targets for the period 2015–2030. These goals aim to create a shared future for all, providing a comprehensive approach that covers almost every aspect of the environment and ecosystem. In particular, SDG 9 offers a broad conceptual framework for identifying areas in manufacturing companies that can significantly contribute to the fourth industrial revolution (Industry 4.0) and the transformation of innovation in contemporary contexts. Industry 4.0 is characterised by the integration of Internet technologies into industrial processes (Drath & Horch, 2014). These technological advances are not only about automation but also about creating networks of machines that are digitally connected and able to communicate and make decentralised decisions.

Considering the Global Sustainable Development Goals, this ninth UN SDG emphasises the importance of sustainable innovation in developing resilient infrastructure, sustainable industrialisation, and fostering innovation. It emphasises the need for sustainable innovation with the aim of increasing resource efficiency

DOI: 10.4324/9781032697895-7

and adopting environmentally friendly technologies and industrial processes (Denoncourt, 2020).

The terms "innovation" and "sustainability" appear frequently, but both escape a clear definitive interpretation. In general, "innovation" is seen as a positive term for different sectors – private, public, and non-profit – and for whole economies, especially in difficult times. However, there is still a significant gap in explaining the mechanisms underlying the creation of successful innovations. This ambiguity is exacerbated in the context of "sustainable innovation", a concept that, despite its intuitive association with positive development, lacks a clear and structured definition. The term suggests the concept of promoting progress that is beneficial, but its exact meaning and application remain open to interpretation.

An analysis of the existing literature reveals a lack of consensus on the precise definition of sustainable innovation, sustainability, and sustainable development. The lack of precise interpretation highlights the complexity and evolving nature of these concepts within the scientific and academic communities (Inigo & Albareda, 2016).

The purpose of this chapter is therefore to discuss conceptual approaches and opportunities for implementing sustainable innovation. The remainder of the chapter is organised as follows. Section 6.2 provides an overview of the definition of sustainable innovation, providing a fundamental understanding of the concept. This is followed by an analysis of the dimensions and attributes of sustainable innovation. Section 6.4 covers best practices in sustainable innovation and critically analyses the role of sustainable innovation. The chapter concludes with a summary of key findings.

6.2 Definitions of sustainable innovation

The terms "sustainability" and "sustainable innovation" are frequently invoked in contemporary discourse. These terms, although commonly associated with long-term "green" and "environmental" considerations, do not have a precise and universally accepted definition. The origin of the term "innovation" is derived from the Latin "novus", meaning novelty or newness. Despite its clear etymological roots, the term "innovation" is not defined uniformly. Historically, Schumpeter (1934) defined innovation as the introduction of new elements or the innovative recombination of existing elements in an industrial context. This definition focused primarily on the genesis of new ideas or inventions rather than their practical implementation.

Innovation is based on a combination of new and existing knowledge that, through a better understanding of business behaviour and processes, can promote sustainable innovation (Grabara et al., 2020). In the literature, the terms "eco-innovation" and "sustainable innovation" are often used interchangeably, despite minor differences in their definitions. Eco-innovation, also known as green, ecological, or environmental innovation, mainly refers to the environmental dimension of sustainable development. Sustainable innovation or sustainability-oriented innovation goes beyond environmental issues and includes social, economic, and environmental aspects (Adams et al., 2016; Calik & Bardudeen, 2016; Rennings, 2000; Sołtysik et al., 2019).

The motivation behind eco-innovations or sustainable innovations is not limited to environmental or social improvements (Carrillo-Hermosilla et al., 2010). These innovations can emerge as by-products of economic motivation, such as cost reduction or increasing market share (Horbach et al., 2012; Urbaniec et al., 2021). As a result, they can be classified as sustainability-motivated innovation or innovation with sustainable benefits (Carrillo-Hermosilla et al., 2010). Importantly, sustainable innovation is necessary to meet environmental and social obligations within a broader framework of sustainable development (Rennings, 2000; Calik & Bardudeen, 2016).

To clarify what sustainable innovation is, Ottosson et al. (2017, p. 191) propose the following definition:

> *a sustainable solution* is a solution that has been developed to be a long-lasting, environmentally responsible solution for the provider (the business), the society and also the users;
>
> *an innovation* is a new solution that has been "sold" and is used by more than one user or that is used in at least one-use situation;
>
> *the innovation process*, done as *an innovation project*, contains all of the stages from idea generation, development (R&D) and commercialization to an implemented solution on the market. (Emphasis added)

Furthermore, sustainable innovations have been defined as "any new or significant improvement of products, services, technological or organizational processes, commercialized or internally implemented that not only provide economic benefits but also generate positive social and environmental impacts".

Sustainable innovation refers to a company's implementation or modification of a new or existing product, process, or practice that results in a significant reduction in the environmental impact of the company's operations. Sustainable innovation is not limited to tangible products, but also encompasses processes and practices, reflecting a comprehensive approach to sustainability (Varadarajan, 2017). In recent years, there has been an increasing emphasis on process and product innovation in the industrial sector. This shift is in line with the move towards development patterns that are sustainable in social, environmental, and economic terms. An important aspect of this transformation is the reconfiguration of process and product innovation to minimise environmental impacts at the production stage, rather than relying solely on consumer measures. The rationale behind the various terms and phrases key to the definition of sustainable innovation is shown in Table 6.1.

The literature increasingly recognises the importance of innovation for survival and growth, especially in highly competitive and uncertain environments (Gunday et al., 2011; Rennings, 2000). Given growing consumer awareness, stringent government regulation, and increasing stakeholder expectations of sustainability, sustainable innovation is becoming a key issue for both corporate actors

Table 6.1 Key elements of the definition of sustainable innovation

Key features	*Rationale*
The implementation of a new or modification of an existing product, process, or practice	It means that sustainable innovation can be a completely new solution or an improvement of something that already exists; it emphasises the ongoing nature of innovation in sustainable development.
Significant reduction in environmental impact	The emphasis here is on the significant positive impact of the innovation on the environment, society, and economy; this can mean, for example, reducing pollution, protecting resources, and increasing the quality of life.
Life cycle environmental impact	This aspect of the definition recognises that the environmental impact of a product does not only occur at the time of its creation or use but covers its entire life cycle; a comprehensive assessment of a product's environmental footprint considers all stages, from resource extraction to disposal.

Source: Own study.

and policymakers (Adams et al., 2016; Doran & Ryan, 2016). Sustainable innovation is defined as innovation that integrates environmental and social dimensions in addition to economic considerations (Adams et al., 2016). There is also a strategic dimension for new companies to be more competitive (Doran & Ryan, 2016). On the one hand, such innovations enable firms to explore new market areas or increase their share of existing markets, as rapid technological advances and intense global competition increasingly reduce the value of existing products and services (Gunday et al., 2011). On the other hand, policymakers can use regulatory frameworks and other instruments to promote sustainable innovation, thereby mitigating environmental issues, enhancing social welfare, and stimulating investment in research and development. In line with the principles of sustainable development, impact assessment should include economic, environmental, and social dimensions. In terms of assessing the impact of sustainable innovations, companies focus on micro-level effects, while policymakers show interest in effects at both meso (specific sectors) and macro levels. To conclude, sustainable innovation has a broad and multifaceted scope that is reflected in the reduction of environmental impacts through both incremental and radical changes in products, processes, and practices.

6.3 Dimensions and attributes of sustainable innovations

The term "sustainability" has become widely used across disciplines, highlighting its interdisciplinary nature (Inigo & Albareda, 2016). This reflects the growing recognition that sustainability encompasses a wide range of issues, from technological innovation and industrial processes to broader environmental, social, and economic factors. Sustainable development thus serves as a guiding framework for aligning different sectors and disciplines to achieve a more sustainable and equitable future.

The concept of sustainable innovation highlights the importance of innovations that address multiple dimensions of sustainability: economic, social, and environmental. Unlike innovations that only introduce new ideas or technologies, sustainable innovation is characterised by its ability to generate positive outcomes in these three key areas, thus making the innovation process more complex and challenging. One of the main challenges in achieving sustainable innovation is the inherent *uncertainty* associated with introducing radical or highly novel ideas (Barbieri et al., 2010). Predicting the economic impact of such innovations is relatively easier, given the availability of various analytical tools and methods designed for this purpose. However, assessing the social and environmental impacts is much more difficult. These areas involve a wider range of variables and uncertainties, as well as complex interactions that can be difficult to estimate and predict (Inigo & Albareda, 2016). In practice, there are many sustainable innovations, each with different attributes, determinants, and impacts on business performance (Adams et al., 2016).

Sustainable innovation has been described as the development of products, services, and processes that, when viewed from a full life-cycle perspective, result in less environmental damage or greater social impact compared with existing alternatives, while taking into account the needs of future generations. Barbieri et al. (2010) argue that contemporary innovation needs to look beyond traditional boundaries and embrace the three dimensions of sustainability and their impacts. These dimensions include:

- economic dimension – concern for economic efficiency, without which companies could not sustain themselves. For companies, this dimension means making profits and generating a competitive advantage in the markets in which they operate. From an *economic* perspective, it is important to note that there are significant contextual differences in the effectiveness of sustainable innovations. As pointed out by Bocken et al. (2014), sustainable innovation can provide market share and competitive advantages across sectors, potentially creating economic disadvantages for those engaged in unsustainable practices. Such a transformation has the potential to initiate significant changes in the global economic landscape, although significant divergence between different industries and national contexts is anticipated. Moreover, recognition of the economic benefits associated with sustainable innovation is expected to gradually permeate the mindset of business owners and investors (Hawn et al., 2018).
- environmental dimension – concern for the environmental impact caused by the use of natural resources and emissions. In the *environmental* field, innovation has significant potential to slow down environmental degradation. However, some countries may still experience less favourable outcomes due to institutional forces or population growth trends. Furthermore, differences in cultural and institutional support for environmental issues in different contexts, as highlighted by Gelissen (2007), are expected to influence the nature of innovations

adopted and their perceived validity. From an empirical point of view, contemporary observations reveal significant divergences in environmental policies and consumption patterns between developed and emerging markets, as well as in the emergence of "eco-innovations" from firms.
- social dimension – concern for the social impact of innovations on human communities within and outside the organisation (unemployment, social exclusion, poverty, etc.; organisational diversity, etc.). In terms of *social* progress, there is an increase in regional polarisation, despite the potential for innovation to promote growth in some previously marginalised areas (Prahalad, 2012). Overall, trajectories in economic, social, and ecological systems are likely to lead to some regions experiencing gains and some societies may move towards greater equality and prosperity, while others may fall into increasingly disadvantaged conditions. The role of innovations in sustainable development is twofold: they can either accelerate these changes or they can contribute to increasing global equity, particularly in aspects such as working conditions and fair wages (Porter & Kramer, 2011).

Sustainable innovation is used as a key instrument to achieve sustainability, defined as the development of processes that keep resource use and waste production within acceptable environmental limits (Li et al., 2017). The systemic nature of sustainable innovation plays a key role in activating innovation systems that foster sustainable development. It is essential for the implementation of comprehensive technical, economic, social, and environmental sustainability, thus creating a "win-win" situation (Kilkis, 2016; Inigo & Albareda, 2016).

Sustainable innovation essentially aims to meet the needs of the current generation without hindering future generations from meeting their needs. The concept encompasses several key attributes, each of which is crucial to its overall impact and effectiveness:

- environmental responsibility – central to sustainable innovation is a commitment to environmental stewardship. This involves reducing resource consumption, minimising waste and pollution, and reducing negative impacts on natural ecosystems. Sustainable innovation encourages the adoption of renewable energy sources, the use of environmentally friendly materials, and the use of advanced technologies that are more efficient and less harmful to the environment (Lubberink et al., 2017).
- social impact – an integral aspect of sustainable innovation is a focus on social factors. It emphasises social justice, inclusivity, and improving the well-being of communities. This dimension of sustainable innovation aims to address social challenges such as poverty, inequality, and limited access to basic services such as education, healthcare, and clean water. It involves creating products or services that significantly improve the quality of life, especially for people in underserved communities (Lubberink et al., 2017).
- renewable energy and clean technologies – innovations in renewable energy, energy storage, and energy efficiency are important elements of sustainable

innovation. These technological advances aim to reduce dependence on fossil fuels, thereby contributing to climate change mitigation (Ebrahim, 2020).

- innovative business models – this aspect of sustainable innovation may involve rethinking traditional business models to prioritise sustainability. This includes models that emphasise shared resources, prioritise access over ownership, and generate value through sustainable practices. Examples include models such as ride-sharing services, renewable energy subscription models, and product-as-a-service offerings (Boons & Lüdeke-Freund, 2013).
- collaboration and partnerships – sustainable innovation often requires multi-stakeholder collaboration, including partnerships between businesses, government entities, non-governmental organisations (NGOs), research institutions, and local communities. Such collaborations can facilitate the pooling of resources, knowledge, and expertise, thereby enabling the development and implementation of sustainable solutions at scale (Reficco et al., 2018).

Each of these features contributes to the overarching goal of sustainable innovation: to create a balance between meeting present needs and preserving the ability of future generations to meet them, thus fostering more sustainable and equitable development. Overall, sustainable innovation requires a holistic approach that goes beyond mere novelty. It requires careful consideration of how new ideas and technologies will affect not only the economy but also society and the environment. Such a holistic view ensures that innovation makes a positive contribution to all these dimensions, aligning with the broader goals of sustainable development.

6.4 Best practices in sustainable innovation

The implementation of sustainable innovation as part of corporate strategies depends on the company's approach to sustainability. Companies can be divided into three distinct groups based on their sustainability strategy and the corresponding extent of innovation in their business models. The first category includes companies that focus on *internal, incremental sustainability* innovation with the aim of mitigating harm, often motivated by regulatory incentives (Adams et al., 2016). These companies typically require minimal to moderate changes to their business models to integrate sustainability strategies (Schaltegger et al., 2012). The second category includes companies that pursue *comprehensive sustainability innovations.* They seek to generate shared value through collaboration with direct stakeholders in the value chain (Adams et al., 2016). These organisations periodically adjust elements of their business models to improve sustainability without fundamentally challenging their core business (Schaltegger et al., 2012). The third category includes companies that work with a wide range of stakeholders to facilitate systemic change, aiming for a net *positive impact through radical sustainability innovation* (Adams et al., 2016). For these companies, sustainability is a key aspect and they are open to deeper transformations in their business models (Schaltegger et al., 2012).

Furthermore, companies can be characterised by their engagement with both internal and external stakeholders, leading to the adoption of two different practices. The first practice focuses on internal stakeholders, namely managers and employees, and includes strategies such as supporting top management, empowering employees, implementing incentives and rewards, fostering collaboration, and ensuring effective communication. The second practice is oriented towards external stakeholders, particularly the supply chain and customers. This includes understanding customers' needs, adopting a proactive approach, initiating early interactions with customers, fostering relationships, communicating effectively, motivating, creating partnerships, and customising or facilitating a variety of services.

Recent trends in the global corporate world point to a growing emphasis on sustainability-oriented innovation as a key determinant of corporate innovation and a crucial element of business strategy. In this context, innovations driven by sustainability aims are increasingly aligned with global challenges such as climate change, resource scarcity, biodiversity degradation, social inequality, and poverty. These innovations are characterised by a focus on developing solutions that simultaneously promote environmental, social, and economic sustainability. This multifaceted approach distinguishes sustainable innovation from traditional innovation models that have historically prioritised economic growth, often at the expense of environmental and social issues.

Sustainable innovation includes a range of practices and technologies that promote environmental stewardship and social responsibility. Key examples of good practice areas for sustainable innovation are shown in Table 6.2.

The growing emphasis on sustainable products and technologies is contributing to the development of sustainable innovations and thus to a greener future. Examples of institutions or initiatives involved in sustainable innovation include:

- the Green Building Initiative (GBI) is an international effort focusing on the development of sustainable and resource-efficient building structures. The initiative includes a certification programme targeting commercial buildings, aligning them with ecologically responsible principles. The main aims of the GBI are to establish a global standard for best practice in green building design and provide external assessment instruments to evaluate compliance with sustainability criteria (https://thegbi.org).
- ENGIE Insight, founded in 1996 in Spokane, Washington, is a leading energy and sustainability management company. Using advanced technology solutions and expert consultation, ENGIE Insight helps companies, including such well-known companies as AMTRAK and GameStop, adopt resource-efficient and environmentally friendly business strategies. The company uses comprehensive data analytics, focusing on consumption, costs, and carbon emissions across multiple utilities, impacting hundreds of thousands of business locations and millions of households. ENGIE Insight's mission is to increase efficiency and sustainability for its customers by offering well-managed, high-tech environmental solutions. These solutions aim not only to reduce risk and improve company reputations but also to increase financial returns (www.engieimpact.com).

Table 6.2 Examples of good practice areas for sustainable innovation

Good practice areas	*Sustainable innovation examples*
Renewable energy technologies	• this involves the development and adoption of clean energy sources such as solar, wind, and hydropower. • these technologies are key to reducing dependence on fossil fuels and tackling climate change.
Circular economy practices	• this approach focuses on designing products that are sustainable, repairable, and recyclable. • it includes strategies to minimise waste, extend the life of products, and increase recycling and reuse of materials.
Sustainable agriculture	• this sector uses state-of-the-art methods such as precision farming, organic farming, agroecology, and vertical farming. • these techniques aim to promote sustainable food production, reduce resource consumption, and protect biodiversity.
Sustainable transport	• innovations in this area include developing electric vehicles, improving public transport systems, and promoting alternative fuels and mobility solutions. • these efforts are key to reducing greenhouse gas emissions and air pollution.
Social enterprises	• these are companies with a core social mission. • examples include fair trade organisations, microfinance institutions, and companies dedicated to providing basic services such as clean water, affordable housing, or educational opportunities in underserved areas

Source: Own study based on Cannas et al. (2020), Koval et al. (2022), and Stenton et al. (2021).

- S.Café has developed a pioneering method of transforming coffee grounds into sustainable fabrics suitable for garments. Their patented yarn, distinguished by its energy-efficient production process, dries much faster than traditional cotton, requiring less energy and lower temperatures for production. The yarn has unique micropores that provide natural odour absorption and UV protection, adding to a range of environmental and functional attributes (https://scafefabrics.com/s-cafe-technology).
- LYSPACKAGING has launched Veganbottle, an innovative and all-natural alternative to bioplastic that is set to revolutionise the future of bottles. Made from 100% biodegradable materials, including the cap and packaging, the Veganbottle's main ingredient is sugar cane extract. This eco-friendly choice not only uses a crop that requires significantly less water but also ensures that the production process uses less energy compared with traditional bottle production. Veganbottle represents a milestone in reducing the use of plastic bottles (https://en.lyspackaging.com).
- Fairphone is launching a modular smartphone, designed in line with fair work practices and promoting recyclability. In response to the growing issue of electronic waste, Fairphone has designed a durable smartphone with an emphasis on ease of repair. This innovative approach allows users to replace specific,

malfunctioning modules instead of throwing away the entire phone. With interchangeable components ranging from the battery to the audio jack, Fairphone aims to significantly reduce the number of phones ending up in landfill (www.fairphone.com/en).
- PulPac, based in Gothenburg, provides fibre-based packaging technology, offering a sustainable and cost-competitive alternative to plastics. The solution is efficient and cost-effective for a variety of applications (www.pulpac.com)
- Oceanium, which operates in Oban, UK, develops and produces innovative, functional seaweed-based ingredients for the food, wellness, and materials sectors, benefiting both people and the health of the oceans. It provides its commercial partners with sustainable ingredients to meet consumer demands and sustainability goals (https://oceanium.world).
- Ecobean, based in Warsaw, is dedicated to increasing the sustainability of the coffee value chain. The company has developed a proprietary technology that transforms coffee grounds waste into sustainable materials and specialised chemicals, solving a global problem while reducing its carbon footprint (https://ecobean.pl).

The above examples illustrate successful sustainable innovation initiatives. The aim of these innovations is to contribute to sustainable development by creating less waste and offering alternatives and more cost-effective solutions. Sustainable innovation, unlike conventional innovation (Boons et al. 2013), involves a wider range of factors. Complexity in this context is defined by Mitchell (2009) as the interconnectedness of a large number of factors. Consequently, the greater number of elements involved makes sustainable innovations more complex than their conventional counterparts. Sustainable innovation projects typically face a wider range of challenges compared with conventional innovation projects (Adams et al. 2016). For sustainable innovations, the integration and management of environmental and social stakeholders need further investigation for these challenges.

Innovations are not without challenges. They can lead to neutral or even negative outcomes in environmental, social, or economic terms. Innovation goes beyond mere technological development; it covers a broader spectrum of impacts. In order for innovations to contribute effectively to the UN's global aims, a comprehensive assessment of their potential impact on social, environmental, and economic dimensions is crucial. This assessment is necessary before introducing new innovations into the market or implementing changes in organisational or production processes.

6.5 Conclusions

Sustainable innovation is currently in the early stages of its development trajectory. The aim of this chapter was to explore the various concepts, challenges, and potential solutions related to sustainable innovation.

Innovation is increasingly recognised as a key driver of sustainable development and the achievement of the United Nations Global Agenda 2030 goals, particularly as highlighted in SDG 9. The importance of innovation lies in its potential to provide significant economic, social, and environmental benefits, positively impacting organisations, society, and the environment. Moreover, the aims of sustainable development open up numerous opportunities for both businesses and society as a whole.

While innovation is increasingly recognised as a key factor for competitive advantage, a growing number of organisations are also seeking to integrate social and environmental considerations into their economic value creation processes. Sustainability in this context involves integrating both environmental and social elements into an organisation's operations and stakeholder engagement. Sustainable companies provide products and services that meet societal needs and positively impact the well-being of the Earth's inhabitants.

The discourse presented here has important implications for both practitioners and researchers. A notable obstacle is the lack of a repository of information on sustainable innovation, making it difficult to deepen their understanding of the field. This scarcity of information "limits research, education and training in this subject area, and hence limits practical experimentation and implementation in industry" (Bocken et al., 2014, p. 44). It is imperative that practitioners recognise that the implementation and evaluation of sustainable innovations is a dynamic learning process that assists in decision-making rather than being the end goal. As the field continues to evolve and transform, cross-industry analyses can yield practical insights. For researchers, the sphere of sustainable innovation provides ample opportunities to formulate and analyse theoretical frameworks.

Furthermore, the development of innovations should be guided by social, environmental, and economic challenges, reinforcing the concept of sustainable innovation. By adhering to this approach, which emphasises the balance of these three pillars – economic viability, social equity, and environmental responsibility – innovation can serve as a powerful tool in achieving the aims of the UN Agenda 2030, thereby contributing to the broader sustainable development goals. This perspective ensures that innovation is not only technologically advanced but also socially and environmentally responsible.

References

Adams, R., Jeanrenaud, S., Bessant, J., Denyer, D., & Overy, P. (2016). Sustainability-oriented innovation: A systematic review. *International Journal of Management Reviews*, *18*(2), 180–205.

Afeltra, G., Alerasoul, S. A., & Strozzi, F. (2023). The evolution of sustainable innovation: From the past to the future. *European Journal of Innovation Management*, *26*(2), 386–421. https://doi.org/10.1108/EJIM-02-2021-0113

Barbieri, J. C., Vasconcelos, I. F. G., Andreassi, T. et al. (2010). Innovation and sustainability: New models and proposition. *Rev Administração Empresas*, *50*, 146–154. https://doi.org/10.1590/S0034-75902010000200002

Baumgartner, R. J. (2011). Critical perspectives of sustainable development research and practice. *Journal of Cleaner Production*, *19*(8), 783–786.

Bocken, N., Short, S. W., Rana, P., & Evans, S. (2014). A literature and practice review to develop sustainable business model archetypes. *Journal of Cleaner Production*, *65*, 42–56.

Boons, F., & Lüdeke-Freund, F. (2013). Business models for sustainable innovation: State-of-the-art and steps towards a research agenda. *Journal of Cleaner Production*, *45*, 9–19.

Boons, F., Montalvo, C., Quist, J., & Wagner, M. (2013). Sustainable innovation, business models and economic performance: An overview. *Journal of Cleaner Production*, *45*, 1–8.

Brundtland, G. H. (1987). *Our common future world commission on environment and development*. UN.

Calik, E., & Bardudeen, F. (2016). A measurement scale to evaluate sustainable innovation performance in manufacturing organizations. *Procedia CIRP*, *40*, 449–454.

Cannas, V. G., Ciccullo, F., Pero, M., & Cigolini, R. (2020). Sustainable innovation in the dairy supply chain: Enabling factors for intermodal transportation. *International Journal of Production Research*, *58*(24), 7314–7333.

Carrillo-Hermosilla, J., Del Río, P., & Könnölä, T. (2010). Diversity of eco-innovations: Reflections from selected case studies. *Journal of Cleaner Production*, *18*(10–11), 1073–1083.

Denoncourt, J. (2020). Companies and UN 2030 sustainable development goal 9 industry, innovation and infrastructure. *Journal of Corporate Law Studies*, *20*(1), 199–235.

Doran, J., & Ryan, G. (2016). The importance of the diverse drivers and types of environmental innovation for firm performance. *Business Strategy and the Environment*, *25*(2), 102–119.

Drath, R., & Horch, A. (2014). Industrie 4.0: Hit or hype?[industry forum]. *IEEE Industrial Electronics Magazine*, *8*(2), 56–58.

Ebrahim, T. Y. (2020). Clean and sustainable technology innovation. *Current Opinion in Environmental Sustainability*, *45*, 113–117.

Gelissen, J. (2007). Explaining popular support for environmental protection: A multilevel analysis of 50 nations. *Environment and Behavior*, *39*(3), 392–415.

Grabara, J., Hussain, H. I., & Szajt, M. (2020). Sustainable university development through sustainable human resources and corporate entrepreneurship: The role of sustainable innovation and work environment. *Amfiteatru Economic*, *22*(54), 480–495. https://doi.org/10.24818/EA/2020/54/480

Gunday, G., Ulusoy, G., Kilic, K., & Alpkan, L. (2011). Effects of innovation types on firm performance. *International Journal of Production Economics*, *133*(2), 662–676.

Hawn, O., Chatterji, A. K., & Mitchell, W. (2018). Do investors actually value sustainability? New evidence from investor reactions to the Dow Jones Sustainability Index (DJSI). *Strategic Management Journal*, *39*(4), 949–976.

Horbach, J., Rammer, C., & Rennings, K. (2012). Determinants of eco-innovations by type of environmental impact—The role of regulatory push/pull, technology push and market pull. *Ecological Economics*, *78*, 112–122.

Inigo, E. A., & Albareda, L. (2016). Understanding sustainable innovation as a complex adaptive system: A systemic approach to the frm. *Journal of Cleaner Production*, *126*, 1–20.

Kilkis, S. (2016). Sustainability-oriented innovation system analyses of Brazil, Russia, India, China, South Africa, Turkey and Singapore. *Journal of Cleaner Production*, *130*, 235–247. https://doi.org/10.1016/j.jclepro.2016.03.138

Koho, M., Torvinen, S., & Romiguer, A. T. (2011). *Objectives, enablers and challenges of sustainable development and sustainable manufacturing: Views and opinions of Spanish companies*. Paper presented at the International Symposium on Assembly and Manufacturing (ISAM).

Koval, V., Arsawan, I. W. E., Suryantini, N. P. S., Kovbasenko, S., Fisunenko, N., & Aloshyna, T. (2022). Circular economy and sustainability-oriented innovation: Conceptual framework and energy future avenue. *Energies*, *16*(1), 243.

Li, D., Zheng, M., Cao, C., Chen, X., Ren, S., & Huang, M. (2017). The impact of legitimacy pressure and corporate profitability on green innovation: Evidence from China top 100.

Journal of Cleaner Production, *141*, 41–49. https://doi.org/10.1016/j.jclepro.2016.08.123
Lubberink, R., Blok, V., Van Ophem, J., & Omta, O. (2017). Lessons for responsible innovation in the business context: A systematic literature review of responsible, social and sustainable innovation practices. *Sustainability*, *9*(5), 721.
Mitchell, S. D. (2009). *Unsimple truths: Science, complexity, and policy*. University of Chicago Press.
Murphy, K. (2012). The social pillar of sustainable development: A literature review and framework for policy analysis. *Sustainability: Science, Practice, and Policy*, *8*(1), 15–29.
Ottosson, S., Moldavska, A., Ogorodnyk, O., & Skogsrød, T. (2017). What is and how to develop sustainable innovation? In *Leadership, innovation and entrepreneurship as driving forces of the global economy: Proceedings of the 2016 International Conference on Leadership, Innovation and Entrepreneurship (ICLIE)* (pp. 191–209). Springer International Publishing.
Porter, M. E., & Kramer, M. R. (2011). Creating shared value. *Harvard Business Review*, *89*(1/2), 62–77.
Prahalad, C. K. (2012). Bottom of the pyramid as a source of breakthrough innovations. *Journal of Product Innovation Management*, *29*(1), 6–12.
Reficco, E., Gutiérrez, R., Jaén, M. H., & Auletta, N. (2018). Collaboration mechanisms for sustainable innovation. *Journal of Cleaner Production*, *203*, 1170–1186.
Rennings, K. (2000). Redefining innovation—Eco-innovation research and the contribution from ecological economics. *Ecological Economics*, *32*(2), 319–332.
Schaltegger, S., Lüdeke, F., & Hansen, E. G. (2012). Business cases for sustainability and the role of business model innovation: Developing a conceptual framework. *International Journal of Innovation and Sustainable Development*, *6*(2), 95–119.
Schumpeter, J. A. (1934). *The theory of economic development: An inquiry into profits, capital, credit, interest, and the business cycle*. Transaction Books.
Sołtysik, M., Urbaniec, M., & Wojnarowska, M. (2019). Innovation for sustainable entrepreneurship: Empirical evidence from the bioeconomy sector in Poland. *Administrative Sciences*, *9*(3), 50.
Stenton, M., Houghton, J. A., Kapsali, V., & Blackburn, R. S. (2021). The potential for regenerated protein fibres within a circular economy: Lessons from the past can inform sustainable innovation in the textiles industry. *Sustainability*, *13*(4), 2328.
Urbaniec, M., Tomala, J., & Martinez, S. (2021). Measurements and trends in technological eco-innovation: Evidence from environment-related patents. *Resources*, *10*(7), 68.
Varadarajan, R. (2017). Innovating for sustainability: A framework for sustainable innovations and a model of sustainable innovations orientation. *Journal of the Academy of Marketing Science*, *45*(1), 14–36. https://doi.org/10.1007/s11747-015-0461-6

7 Sustainable project management

Sustainability refers to the ability to sustain natural processes, objects, and matter in which competing forces can coexist in due balance. The continuous overexploitation of certain resources or matter causes them to be depleted, thus causing an imbalance and eventually exhaustion (Liu, 2017). Sustainable development, on the other hand, is treated as a long-term goal, resulting from the processes implemented within the framework of sustainable development (UNESCO, 2021).

The concept of sustainable development is still being developed, moving to the organisational level (Baumgartner & Ebner, 2010; Dyllick &, 2016) and tailored to different fields of knowledge, such as entrepreneurship (Hall et al., 2010; Schaltegger & Wagner, 2011; Shepherd & Patzelt, 2011), knowledge management (Martins et al., 2019; López-Torres et al., 2019), human resource management (Ehnert, 2009; Wagner, 2011; Macke & Genari, 2019), and finally, project management (Chawla et al., 2018; Armenia et al., 2019).

As a result of the triple structure, sustainability mainly goes hand in hand with projects that consume large amounts of energy and materials, and their results have a lifelong impact on the environment, society, and the economy (Armenia et al., 2019). However, environmental financial performance relates to the problem of proper resource management within the project life cycle (Silvius & Schipper, 2014), which applies to all types of resources and all types of projects. Proper resource management also has an impact on the bottom line. From the perspective of the processes that make up project management, the above-mentioned activities should be undertaken, including, for example, the development of technology.

Sustainability aspects should be taken into account by sponsors in their decision-making processes regarding the financing of projects. It requires thinking long term about the results of the project. Gareis et al. (2011) stressed the need for a value orientation for all project stakeholders. Sustainable project management should be based on ensuring that all decisions are made in the best interests of stakeholders, including the client and/or end user, the project manager and project team members, the sponsor, and wider society (Silvius & Schipper, 2014). However, the customer is always the most important stakeholder, and value creation requires customer participation (Mustak et al., 2013). A strong relationship with the customer fosters trust and allows for an open discussion of all problems and opportunities.

DOI: 10.4324/9781032697895-8

Sustainability assessment can be carried out at different levels, for example, national and regional, as well as organisational. Organisational sustainability was defined by Dyllice and Hockerts (2002) as "meeting the needs of the direct and indirect stakeholders of the company (such as shareholders, employees, customers, pressure groups, communities, etc.), without prejudice to its ability to meet the needs of future stakeholders".

The company's sustainability policy should be reflected in all functions (e.g., marketing, HR), processes, and projects. However, the effective implementation of sustainability principles in a function, process, or project can act as a stimulus for organisational transformation towards sustainability (Figure 7.1). The implementation of the sustainability paradigm must include an assessment of the following:

- long-term changes to existing technology.
- long-term costs and availability of utilities.
- long-term availability of materials.
- long-term operability and ease of maintenance of process equipment.

Despite recognising the role of projects in the transformation of organisations and society towards sustainable development (Marcelino-Sádaba et al., 2015) and the impact of sustainability concepts on project management, the role of project management in this development remains unexplored. Project management is the link between an organisation's strategy and projects (Too & Weaver, 2014). Project management should provide oversight and assurance and ensure that projects contribute to the achievement of the organisation's strategic goals and perform well and in line with that strategy. Project management should therefore also ensure that projects "reflect the organization's commitment to ethical values and sustainability" (ISO 21505:1017; 201).

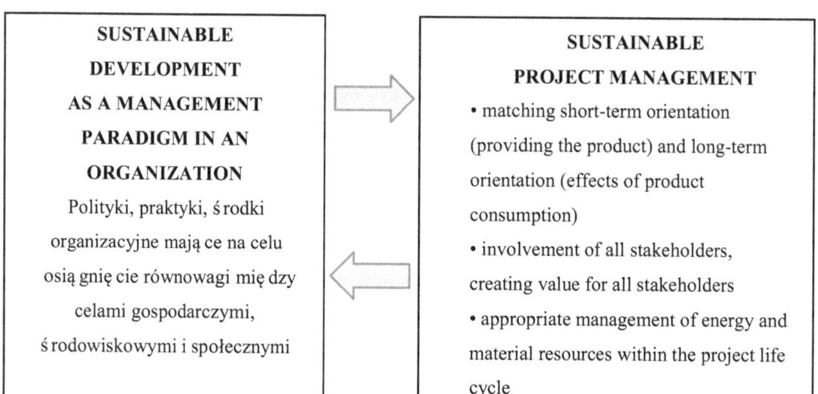

Figure 7.1 Sustainable project management as a result and/or driver of sustainable organisational development.

Simply put, sustainable project management can be defined as

> planning, monitoring and controlling the implementation and support processes of a project, taking into account the environmental, economic and social aspects of the life cycle of the project's resources, processes, deliverables and outcomes, aimed at achieving stakeholder benefits and executed in a transparent, fair and ethical manner that includes proactive stakeholder participation. (Silvius & Schipper, 2014)

The analyses conducted by Wawak and Woźniak indicate that sustainable project management is one of the three new growth trends visible in publications discussing project management. This trend highlights the growing role of sustainable development, mainly in infrastructure and development projects. These projects use a significant amount of resources that can negatively impact the environment, so the sustainability discussion in these projects is geared towards the environmental bottom line (Labuschagne et al., 2005). However, in other types of projects, you can implement durability assumptions.

You can also find links between sustainability and traditional project management. For example, according to the PMBoK, streamlining takes the form of resource balancing to balance the workforce that facilitates the use of resources. PMBoK defines stakeholders as "persons and organisations which are actively involved in the project or whose interests may be positively or negatively affected as a result of the implementation of the project or the successful completion of the project" (Project Management Institute, 1996). Project stakeholder management includes stakeholder identification, stakeholder engagement planning, management, and monitoring of their involvement. Previous research, however, shows that the traditional method of stakeholder management still prevails, even though it should give way to stakeholder engagement from a sustainability perspective (Karlsen, 2002).

It is important to note that Agile is more sustainable than traditional approaches. It provides an answer to the first research question. First, the Agile methodology puts more emphasis on teamwork and stakeholder engagement, which significantly increases the importance of the social aspect, which is also one of the pillars of sustainable development. In addition, one of the common elements of Agile project management and sustainability is complexity. The theory suggests that when dealing with a complex project, it must be managed in an Agile manner. According to Messiah (2016), sustainability is associated with complexity, for example, in the context of socio-political or ecological systems and their interactions. Other common points for Agile and sustainable project management include long-term orientation, stakeholder interests, and value orientation (Khizar et al., 2021).

Interpretations of sustainability in project management can be divided into three groups. The first group embodies attempts to develop comprehensive classical definitions (*definiendum-definins*). Two examples can be cited. The first is synthetic: "Sustainability in the design profession is an approach to business that balances the environmental, social, and economic aspects of project-based work to meet the current needs of stakeholders without compromising or unduly burdening future generations" (APM, 2019). The second was proposed by Silvius et al. (2016, p. 40): "Sustainability in projects and project management is the development, delivery, and management of a project-organized change in policies, processes, resources, assets, or organizations, taking into account the six principles of sustainability in a project, its outcomes, and outcomes".

The second group includes definitions/interpretations based on enumerations of the characteristics of the relationship between project management and sustainability. As a first example, the comprehensive description of the sustainability bases of the project proposed by Morfawa (2014) was cited. This interpretation covers virtually all project characteristics, for example, project sustainability dimensions, sustainability elements, sustainable business examples, project sustainability characteristics, project sustainability measurement, and project sustainability management. In a similar trial, Chawla et al. (2018, p. 164) identified general parameters to measure sustainability in projects: profitability, safety, transparency, ethics, nature-friendliness, social acceptance, and meeting stakeholder and customer expectations.

As in the case above, this interpretation also includes a third, holistic approach to the practice and theory of sustainable development in project management and is presented by leading authors in the field. Taking as a starting point the universal interpretations of sustainable development and the characteristics of the relationship between management and sustainable development, they developed a logically coherent concept showing the relationship between sustainability and project management.

The second structure of research on the relationship of Agile (agility), complexity, and sustainability with projects and project management includes normative, purposeful, persuasive, and performative interpretations of these terms. It also refers to management in a universal sense. Of course, this order is arbitrary to some extent, but it allows for a preliminary systematisation of the importance of Agile (agile and agility), complexity, and sustainability in projects and project management.

Agile in its meaning taken from software development, as embodying agility in projects and project management, has a strong normative meaning. A brief explanation of this situation, based on our earlier discussion, stems from the dominance of Agile and agility as patterns of adaptation to a turbulent environment and the need for learning, flexibility, and adaptability in projects and project management. Interpreting Agile as moderately intentional statements means that the goal of achieving higher levels of agility can only be defined in general terms. The high persuasive importance of Agile is a direct result of its strong normative sense and importance in projects and project management. The poor performativity of the terms Agile and agility is due to the very strong influence of emergence and self-organisation.

Seen from this perspective, it is easy to conclude that sustainability in its interpretations across the social scale is always highly positive. However, it is natural that it cannot be created solely by declarations. An interesting phenomenon can be observed in sustainability research. Seen from this perspective, it is easy to conclude that sustainability in its interpretations across the social scale is always highly positive. However, it is natural that it cannot be created solely by declarations.

References

Armenia, S., Dangelico, R. M., Nonino, F., & Pompeii, A. (2019). Sustainable project management: A conceptualization-oriented review and framework proposal for future research. *Sustainability*, *11*(9), 2664. https://doi.org/10.3390/su11092664

Association for Project Management (APM). (2019). *APM body of knowledge*. Project Sustainability. https://www.apm.org.uk/resources/what-is-project-management/what-is-sustainability-in-project-management/

Baumgartner, R. J., & Ebner, D. (2010). Corporate sustainability strategies: Sustainability profiles and maturity levels. *Sustainable Development*, *18*(2), 76–89. https://doi.org/10.1002/sd.447

Chawla, V. K., Chandab, A. K., Angra, S., & Chawla, G. R. (2018). The sustainable project management: A review and future possibilities. *Journal of Project Management*, *3*, 157–170.

Dyllick, T., & Hockerts, K. (2002). More than a business case for corporate sustainability. *Business Strategy and the Environment*, *11*(2), 130–141. https://doi.org/10.1002/bse.323

Dyllick, T., & Muff, K. (2016). Explaining the importance of sustainable business. *Organization and Environment*, *29*(2), 156–174. https://doi.org/10.1177/1086026615575176

Ehnert, I. (2009). *Sustainable human resource management: A conceptual and exploratory analysis from a paradox*. Physica-Verlag HD.

Gareis, R., Huemann, M., & Martinuzzi, A. (2011). What can project management learn from sustainability principles? *Project Perspectives*, *XXXII*, 60–65.

Hall, J. K., Daneke, G. A., & Lenox, M. J. (2010). Sustainability and entrepreneurship: Past contributions and future directions. *Journal of Business Venturing*, *25*(5), 439–448. https://doi.org/10.1016/j.jbusvent.2010.01.002

Institute of Project Management. (1996). *Project management knowledge body*. Project Management Institute.

ISO 21505:1017; Project, programme and portfolio management: Guidance on governance. International Organization for Standardization.

Karlsen, J. T. (2002). Project stakeholder management. *Engineering Management Journal*, *14*(4), 19–24. https://doi.org/10.1080/10429247.2002.11415180

Khizar, H. M. U., Iqbal, M. J., & Rasheed, M. I. (2021). Business orientation and sustainability: A systematic review of the literature on sustainability orientation and future research pathways. *Sustainability*. https://doi.org/10.1002/sd.2190

Labuschagne, C., Brent, A. C., & van Erck, R. P. G. (2005). Assessing the sustainability performance of industries. *Journal of Cleaner Production*, *13*(4), 373–385. https://doi.org/10.1016/j.jclepro.2003.10.007

Liu, S. (2017). Sustainable development. In *Bioprocess Engineering* (pp. 829–870). https://doi.org/10.1016/B978-0-444-63783-3.00014-9

López-Torres, G. C., Garza-Reyes, J. A., Maldonado-Guzmán, G., Kumar, V., Rocha-Lona, L., & Cherrafi, A. (2019). Knowledge management for sustainability in operations. *Production Planning and Control*, *30*(10–12), 813–826. https://doi.org/10.1080/09537287.2019.1582091

Macke, J., & Genari, D. (2019). A systematic review of the literature on sustainable human resource management. *Journal of Cleaner Production*, *208*, 806–815. https://doi.org/10.1016/j.jclepro.2018.10.091

Marcelino-Sádaba, S., González-Jaen, L. F., & Pérez-Ezcurdia, A. (2015). Using project management as a way to sustainability: From a comprehensive review to a framework definition. *Journal of Cleaner Production*, *99*, 1–16.

Martins, V. W. B., Rampasso, I. S., Anholon, R., Quelhas, O. L. G., & Leal Filho, W. (2019). Knowledge management in the context of sustainable development: A review of the literature and opportunities for future research. *Journal of Cleaner Production*, *229*, 489–500. https://doi.org/10.1016/j.jclepro.2019.04.354

Messiah, C., Bartusik, K., Małkus, T., & Sołtysik, M. (2022). *Agile project management and complexity: A reappraisal.* Routledge/Taylor & Francis Group.

Morfaw, J. (2014). Fundamentals of project sustainability. Paper presented at PMI® Global Congress 2014, Phoenix, AZ. Newtown Square, PA: Project Management Institute. https://www.pmi.org/learning/library/fundamentals-project-sustainability-9369

Mustak, M., Jaakkola, E., & Halinen, A. (2013). Customer participation and value creation: A systematic review and research implications. *Managing Service Quality: An International Journal*, *23*(4), 341–359. https://doi.org/10.1108/MSQ-03-2013-0046

Schaltegger, S., & Wagner, M. (2011). Sustainable entrepreneurship and innovation in sustainable development: Categories and interactions. *Business Strategy and and the Environment*, *20*(4), 222–237. https://doi.org/10.1002/bse.682

Shepherd, D. A., & Patzelt, H. (2011). A new field of sustainable entrepreneurship: The study of entrepreneurial activities that combine 'what is to be sustainable' with 'what is to be developed'. *Entrepreneurship: Theory and Practice*. https://doi.org/10.1111/j.1540-6520.2010.00426.x

Silvius, A. J. G., & Schipper, R. P. (2014). Sustainability in project management competences: Analysing the competence gap of project managers. *Journal of Human Resource and Sustainability Studies*, *2*(2), 40–58.

Too, E. G., & Weaver, P. (2014). The management of project management: A conceptual framework for project governance. *International Journal of Project Management*, *32*(8), 1382–1394.

UNESCO. https://en.unesco.org/themes/education-sustainable-development/what-is-esd/sd, date; 19.07.2021

Villanen, H. (2014). Teachers' reflections on an education for sustainable development project. *International Research in Geographical and Environmental Education*, *23*(2), 179–191. http://doi.org/10.1080/10382046.2014.908526

Wagner, M. (2011). Environmental management and sustainable human resource management activities in German manufacturing companies – Prevalence, determinants and results | Umweltmanagementaktivitäten und nachhaltiges HRM in Unternehmen des deutschen Verarbeitenden Gewerbes - Verbreitung, Bestimmungsf. *Zeitschrift für Personalforschung*, *25*(2), 157–177. https://doi.org/10.1688/1862-0000_ZfP_2011_02_Wagner

Wawak, S., & Woźniak, K. (2020). The evolution of project management studies in the 21st century. *International Journal of Managing Projects in Business*, *13*(4), 867–888. https://doi.org/10.1108/IJMPB-01-2020-0002

Conclusions

This monograph provides a comprehensive exploration of sustainable transformation in key business areas. The authors begin their analysis by emphasising that despite extensive research and publications in recent years, sustainable development remains poorly recognised in terms of best business practices.

The central thesis of the monograph is that achieving sustainable development goals, in line with the 2030 Agenda for Sustainable Development, depends on research, innovation, and investment in technology and new business models. The authors highlight that companies can gain a competitive advantage by meeting economic, social, and environmental requirements.

The latest research presented in the monograph demonstrates that sustainable business strategies impact the sustainable development of organisations. By aligning their operations with sustainable resource management and developing environmentally friendly products, companies can achieve a competitive edge. However, the authors acknowledge existing challenges for companies in strategic development, particularly in finding a balance between maximising profits and environmental responsibility.

The book has two main research objectives: first, to contribute to a better understanding of significant trends in sustainable transformation in key business areas, and second, to provide a comprehensive review of quantitative and qualitative research in this field. The authors aim to answer research questions on how companies implement sustainable development transformation strategies in their key business areas.

The monograph consists of seven chapters, each focusing on a different aspect of sustainable development in business. The first chapter addresses sustainable transformation as a key goal for organisations in the context of technological progress and climate change. It also emphasises the need for collaboration between societal sectors to achieve sustainable development.

Subsequent chapters delve into specific issues such as designing sustainable business, creating sustainable products, sustainable marketing, entrepreneurship and innovation, and sustainable project management. The authors analyse various aspects of these areas, underscoring the importance of shifting business approaches to incorporate economic, social, and environmental aspects.

Chapters on sustainable marketing and entrepreneurship and innovation highlight that companies, in pursuing sustainable development, should be guided by

DOI: 10.4324/9781032697895-9

social responsibility, creating new products and services that simultaneously support the natural environment and offer economic benefits.

An essential element of the monograph is the examination of sustainable innovation, recognised as a crucial part of business strategy. The authors stress that innovations grounded in ethical, social, economic, and environmental principles can lead to organisational structural changes and contribute to sustainable development.

In summary, the book provides a comprehensive approach to the topic of sustainable development in business, covering diverse aspects from product design to project management. The authors analyse the challenges posed to companies due to the necessity of adapting to sustainable business practices while emphasising the competitive advantages that companies can gain by embracing these challenges.

Index

FSC
www.fsc.org
MIX
Papier | Fördert
gute Waldnutzung
FSC® C083411

Kolibri 360 GmbH
Ferdinand-Jühlke-Straße 7
99095 Erfurt, Deutschland
produktsicherheit@kolibri360.de